FACING VIOLENCE

Discussion-Starting Skits for Teenagers

R. William Pike

Resource Publications, Inc.
San Jose, California

For Ann

Editorial director: Kenneth Guentert
Managing editor: Elizabeth J. Asborno
Copyeditor: Leila T. Bulling

Reprint Department
Resource Publications, Inc.
160 E. Virginia Street #290
San Jose, CA 95112-5876

Library of Congress Cataloging in Publication Data
Pike, R. William.
    Facing violence : discussion-starting skits for teenagers /
R. William Pike.
        p.   cm. (Acting it out)
    Includes index.
    ISBN 0-89390-344-2 (pbk.)
    1. Violence—Prevention. 2. Violence—Juvenile drama.
    3. Teenagers—Conduct of life—Juvenile drama. I. Title. II. Series.
HM291.P4895   1995
303.6—dc20   95-4932

Printed in the United States of America

99 98 97 96 95 | 5 4 3 2 1

Contents

Violence & Dating

Violence & Bias

Violence in Society

Violence & Solutions

Introduction

I began doing research for this book in the summer of 1994. Before I started, I was afraid that I wasn't going to be able to find current information that specifically linked adolescents and violence. I was interested in violence as it pertained to teenagers at home, at school, in relationships, and in society, and I remembered only a few specific articles I had read or documentaries I had seen that addressed these topics. About a week into my research, the media floodgates opened. "Violence and teenagers" was suddenly a hot topic. Everyone from *People* magazine to *Hard Copy* began covering this "new phenomenon." Each week, newspaper headlines would shout out new stories about teenagers and violence: "Cops: Teen Tried to Plot Dad's Death," "2 Boys Pull Gun, Rob Teacher of $4G," "Throwaway Youth," "Kids Killing Kids," "Teens Mourn Classmate Slain at ATM," "2 Teen-Age Robbers Face Exiles in Alaska."

I was amazed that this topic suddenly seemed to be generating so much attention. I began to ask myself several questions: Were there always so many stories chronicling this issue? Had I simply overlooked all the attention in the past? Most important, was the issue of violence and teenagers as new and unusual a problem as many of these stories implied?

In attempting to answer these questions, I stumbled on several important ideas that actually captured the essence of *Facing Violence*. First, it is important to view teenage violence as the *symptom of a problem* rather than as the problem itself. It is easy to look at teenage gangs and deplore the violence they foster, and not many people would disagree with high school principals when they argue that students who were repeatedly

1

fighting at school should be removed from the school population (at least for a short time). After all, we do not want violent students in our classrooms.

A concern emerges, however, when we think we have successfully dealt with these situations after we have dealt with their violence, after we have arrested the violent gang member or suspended the violent student. What some people fail to recognize is that the violence of these situations is merely the tough outer layer of other, deeper problems. They fail to see that the violence is a symptom of a problem, not the problem itself.

To address violence, we ultimately must peel back the layers and address the issues prompting the violent behavior. A few of the issues that prompt violent behavior are:

- intolerance
- prejudice
- racism
- ignorance
- lack of self-esteem
- poverty
- substance abuse

Every violent situation is "layered" differently. In one case, poverty may lead to low self-esteem which in turn may lead to violent behavior. In another case, ignorance may lead to racism which may lead to violent behavior. The combinations are almost limitless, but their result is always the same: violence. As a society, we would be fooling ourselves if we thought that we were solving the problem of violence by only addressing violent behavior while ignoring any underlying causes.

Another idea I quickly came to realize is that, despite what the media want us to believe, the pairing of adolescents and violence is not a "new phenomenon." In fact, the specific issue of adolescent violence in school is deeply rooted in the early civil rights movement. In her book *Warriors Don't Cry* (Pocket Books, 1994), Melba Pattillo Beals powerfully captures her experience as one fo the nine African-American teenagers who integrated Central High School in Little Rock, Arkansas, in 1957. Beals tells the story of a fifteen-year-old high school girl who faced physical violence, verbal attacks, and angry mobs everyday she attended the previously all-white high school. Not only does the story of her bravery add a historical perspective to the issue of teenagers and violence, but it also reinforces the concept that violence is a symptom rather than a problem. Clearly, the violence Beals suffered as a teenager at the hands of other teenagers was a symptom of the racism of the times. Without addressing that racism, there was little hope of ending the violence for any significant time.

Facing Violence helps teenagers confront the violence in their own lives by "peeling back the layers" of violent situations. The book strives to reveal the underlying causes of violence, to provoke discussion about those causes, and to provide examples of positive ways to handle violent situations. Its scenes, monologues, and group orals present situations that are both violent and problematic. They have been written to honestly reflect the many conflicts adolescents face in their lives every day, but they do not offer any simple or "pat" solutions. In fact, in many of the scenes, it is difficult to distinguish "the good guys" from "the bad guys."

This intentional ambiguity accomplishes several important objectives. First, it demonstrates to the reader that every violent situation is unique and that there is never only one right way to behave or only one path to take toward the resolution of a conflict. Second, the ambiguity prompts discussion: "Who's right?" "Who's wrong?" "He shouldn't have done that!" "She should have done this!" Discussion is the heart of *Facing Violence*; when the reader defends the actions of one character or vilifies the actions of another, s/he will begin to form her/his own views on violence. A few discussion questions at the end of each scene have been provided to facilitate lively, but controlled, dialogues.

Unfortunately, there will always be violence and violent people in our society, but perhaps, when more adolescents confront the violence in their lives, discuss it with their families, and argue about it with their friends, they will begin to gain their own insights into the causes of the violence they see around them. With these insights, they can then begin to move us all toward the elimination of ignorance and the celebration of tolerance.

I would like to thank Dr. Susan Finkelstein, an old friend and a gifted child psychiatrist, for carefully going over the manuscript in search of any errors I may have made or of any unintentional messages I may have conveyed. I would also like to thank Ann for her constant support and encouragment.

About the "Stage Directions"

This book is designed to be used on an impromptu basis—without props or preparation—in a classroom and small-group setting. Detailed stage directions are included mainly to help readers better imagine the characters, their personalities, and their actions. When reading the scenes aloud, assign someone the job of reading all the stage directions. Reading the stage directions aloud will help the group to grasp the dynamics of the scene and to better understand the information it conveys. Of course, the stage directions can help organized peer theater groups prepare more elaborate productions.

Violence
in Schools

Journal 10/17

Topic
weapons in school

Character
Teenager (male or female)

> TEENAGER *is writing in a marble notebook and speaking aloud.*

TEENAGER: School sucks. My house sucks. Life sucks.

The only thing I have that's worth anything is this stupid journal. I knew I was going to write in it every day, but things kinda got out of hand. I sort of lost track of time, you know? Anyway, I made the last entry on 9/3, the first day of school. Things can sure change in a month.

9/3. I was so, what's that word, "optimistic." Yeah, I was optimistic. The first day of school, a new start, new beginning. Wrong, again!

One thing that's different is that I've started to carry this razor in my backpack. It's not a real razor, not a major blade or anything, it's just the kind that you use to open cardboard boxes and stuff. I got it at a hardware store a couple weeks ago. It makes me feel...I don't know...It makes me feel safer, I guess. It's not like I'm going to attack somebody or that I'm gonna get tough and start hassling people...It's just good to know it's there.

I know what they're all gonna say: "If the principal finds that thing you could get suspended" or "If your mother finds out, she is going to beat the crap out of you."

Right. Tell me something I don't know. My mother has been beating the crap out of me since I was nine—right after Dad died and she started *really* drinking heavy. I don't need no social worker to tell me the connection there. I'm used to it now. I'm used to her getting smashed and taking her messed-up life out on me.

I wonder if that's why I got the razor?

Listen to me! Now *I'm* sounding like a social worker.

(*Imitating a social worker*) It is my professional opinion that because you have been raised in an abusive and alcoholic environment, you feel scared and threatened. Hence, you have begun to carry a weapon.

No shit?

Anyway, it's not a weapon, it's a razor blade. Calm down! Its only October. You got ten months to go to stay out of trouble...You can do it...You can do it...It's only a razor blade from a hardware store, nothing serious.

Discussion

1. Why do you think Pat believes that the journal is worth something?

2. What feeling does carrying the razor give Pat?

3. What is the connection between the razor and Pat's mother?

4. Do you think a razor is a weapon? Explain.

5. What is meant by the word "rationalization"? How does this word apply to Pat?

6. What do *you* worry Pat might do with the razor?

The Way I See It

Topic
teacher-student violence

Characters
Mr. Goodwin, an English teacher
Joe, a junior in Mr. Goodwin's English class

> JOE *and* MR. GOODWIN *are standing on opposite sides of the stage. They speak directly to the audience.*

MR. GOODWIN: It all happened so fast that I don't know where to begin...

JOE: It all happened so fast that I don't know where to begin...

BOTH: ...but I know that it was his fault.

MR. GOODWIN: He has been a problem since the first day of school, a real wise-ass, you know the type.

JOE: He has hated me since the first day of school. He thought he knew who the trouble-makers and the butt-kissers were, you know the type.

MR. GOODWIN: The first day of class he walks in late and slams his books down on his desk. I looked up and told him that if he ever did that again that he would be in the office in ten seconds flat.

JOE: On the first day of class I was about thirty seconds late because I couldn't find the room. My schedule said room 130 and he was in room 131. I was going to tell him about it but he yelled at me for putting my books down too loud—for putting my books down too loud!

MR. GOODWIN: I could tell he was trouble by just looking at him. He always seemed to be smirking at me. He always seemed to be daring me to catch him doing something wrong. Well, I kept my eye on him.

JOE: He was always staring at me. The second week of school I asked him why he was always staring at me. He ignored me or pretended that he didnt hear my question, so I said, "Why don't you just take a picture!" He didn't have any trouble hearing that. He threw me out of class.

MR. GOODWIN: He started wising off the second week of school and I threw him out. I called his parents and told them about the problem and his father seemed very supportive. He said he would speak with him. After that, he was really pretty good in class.

JOE: When he called home, my father threw a fit. He grounded me for a week. I tried to tell him that Goodwin hated me and had it in for me, but my father wouldn't listen. He said that "the teacher was the teacher" and whatever he said goes. I told him he wasn't being fair. He told me to just behave myself in class. And I did.

MR. GOODWIN: You know, when he puts his mind to it, Joe can do very well in class. He's a bright boy. Unfortunately, his behavior interferes with his learning. We were getting on pretty well in class when this happened.

JOE: I was really trying to do my best. I did all the homework, I answered questions in class, I even volunteered to read aloud! Shakespeare! I hate Shakespeare and it was during a quiz on *Othello* when all this started.

MR. GOODWIN: I was testing the class on the relationship between Iago and Roderigo. You see, Iago would let Roderigo take the blame for everything that was going wrong. I was writing the essay question on the board when I saw a paper airplane fly across the room. It originated, of course, from Joe's corner.

JOE: I was sitting next to Wally Golding when he told me he wasn't writing an essay on this crap. He folded up the paper and threw it across the room. Goodwin saw the plane but didn't see who threw it. He told us to behave ourselves and started to write on the board again. That's when Wally took my paper and threw another plane.

MR. GOODWIN: He even had the nerve to throw a second paper airplane after my warning! I demanded to know who threw the plane. No one said a word.

JOE: I couldn't say that Wally did it, even if he did take my paper.

MR. GOODWIN: I said, "I will find out who is wasting paper and disobeying me and will promptly throw him out of class!"

JOE: That was it. Everyone started to write the essay. But I had one small problem: I didn't have any composition paper. Wally didn't care because he refused to do the essay. But I didn't want to fail. So I went up to Goodwin's desk to get another piece.

MR. GOODWIN: I knew I would get him! He came up to my desk for paper. He asked me if he could take another piece and I just glared at him, shaking my head. "Well, well, well. If we hadn't made all those little airplanes we would have paper for our essay, wouldn't we?"

JOE: I really felt stupid standing up there with him blaming me for something that I didn't do, so I just started to take the paper. That's when he grabbed my arm and shouted, "Put that down, you pain in the ass!"

MR. GOODWIN: He just grabbed the paper off my desk and deliberately disobeyed me! I had to stop him! I said, "You're turning into a real wise-ass, aren't you?""

JOE: That's when I lost it.

MR. GOODWIN: That's when he began to resist.

JOE: I tried to get him to let go but he squeezed my arm tighter. I said, "You better let me go" and I struggled to get away. I remember he was saying, "Or what? Or what?" kinda like he was challenging me to hit him or something.

MR. GOODWIN: He really began to struggle and I became worried that he was going to hurt himself so I held him securely and took him out of the room. I didn't want him to hurt any of the other students.

JOE: Then he freaked out. He twisted my arm behind my back and then he grabbed my hair. He was trying to get me out of the room. When he got me to the door he kinda flung me out and I fell into the hall.

MR. GOODWIN: When I removed him from class, I immediately called for an administrator. I believe that if I hadn't acted quickly, someone would have gotten hurt.

JOE: Look, I have bruises on my arm where he grabbed me and my knee is all messed up from falling in the hall. Teachers just can't beat kids up, can they?

MR. GOODWIN: Students can't endanger other students, can they? I'm sorry that his parents are making such a big deal out of this.

JOE: I'm sorry that I didn't bash him in the face when I had the chance.

MR. GOODWIN: Now I hear his parents are suing.

JOE: My dad told me not to talk about this at school.

MR. GOODWIN: My attorney has advised me not to discuss the matter with anyone. But, I'll tell you one thing...

BOTH: ...he won't get away with this!

Discussion

1. Should Joe have explained that Wally Golding was the person responsible for throwing the paper?

2. Does the teacher over-react? How? What would you have done had you been the teacher?

3. Does Joe over-react? Why do you think they both get so upset?

4. Who is responsible for making the problem worse? Why?

Jimmy St. Louis

Topic
gangs

Characters
Mrs. Paul, a guidance counselor
Mrs. St. Louis, mother of Jimmy, a junior in high school

> MRS. PAUL *has asked* MRS. ST. LOUIS *to come to school to discuss her son. It seems that over the past several months Jimmy has been getting into trouble, missing quite a bit of school, and failing most of his classes.*

MRS. PAUL: Thank you for coming in, Mrs. St. Louis. I've been concerned about Jimmy for some time now and I thought that we had better get together to try to help him get out of this slump he seems to be in. Before we address any specific problems, could you fill me in on his background?

MRS. ST. LOUIS: What do you mean?

MRS. PAUL: Could you tell me a little more about when he was younger? Was he a good student? What's it like at home? Who are his friends? That sort of thing.

MRS. ST. LOUIS: I see. Well, Jimmy was always a good boy. His brothers were a little crazy at times, but Jimmy always did his schoolwork and stayed out of trouble. I remember that when he was in fifth grade he came home and announced that he was going to be a veterinarian! "A veterinarian?" I said. He said, "Yup, that's what I'm going to be." I knew that he was going to be special. I just knew it.

MRS. PAUL: When did you notice a change?

MRS. ST. LOUIS: I suppose I noticed a difference in him when he quit that job he had in the neighborhood last year. He used to work in a deli and one day he just quit. I asked him why and he said something about not paying enough.

MRS. PAUL: Did he look for another job?

MRS. ST. LOUIS: No, he didn't. He started hanging out with this group of boys. They were trouble. I didn't like it at all.

MRS. PAUL: What didn't you like about it?

MRS. ST. LOUIS: Well, all they used to talk about was clothes and sneakers. Buying this and getting that. "Get a job," I told him. "I don't need a job," he said.

MRS. PAUL: What did he mean?

MRS. ST. LOUIS: At first I didn't know, but I had my suspicions. I hoped I was wrong.

MRS. PAUL: You were afraid he was stealing what he wanted?

MRS. ST. LOUIS: That and...You see, my husband and I both work. I am a secretary for a law firm and my husband works for the city. We have given Jimmy everything. Maybe we couldn't afford some of the luxuries the other kids had, but we taught him it was wrong to steal and to rob people.

MRS. PAUL: You think that's what this group of boys does?

MRS. ST. LOUIS: Yes, I do. And it's not "group of boys" anymore. It's a gang.

MRS. PAUL: You're saying your son is part of an organized gang?

MRS. ST. LOUIS: Yes, I am. He started getting home real late at night and when I would go to wake him up in the morning he wouldn't budge. I would keep asking him to get up but then I had to leave for work. When he did get up, I had teachers calling me saying he was sleeping in class. They told me he was failing when he should be getting straight A's.

MRS. PAUL: Didn't you try to get him to come home at a reasonable time?

MRS. ST. LOUIS: We did. We tried everything. Finally, we would lock the door after eleven p.m. and refuse to open it. The first couple of times he would bang on it. Three weeks ago, he stopped coming home.

MRS. PAUL: You haven't seen your son in three weeks?

MRS. ST. LOUIS: Oh, he came home once last week to get his CD player. That's the last time I saw him before it happened.

MRS. PAUL: Before what happened?

MRS. ST. LOUIS: They didn't tell you? I thought you knew.

MRS. PAUL: Knew what?

MRS. ST. LOUIS: (*Struggling*) Two nights ago he was arrested.

MRS. PAUL: On what charge?

MRS. ST. LOUIS: (*Upset*) Robbery. The police said that Jimmy and his...gang...would rob elderly people—

old people! People who couldn't fight back! They would surround them, rough them up, and take their money. A few of the old people wound up in the hospital with broken arms or bad bruises. I can't believe that my son would...

MRS. PAUL: (*Comforting her*) It's all right. Have you gone to the jail yet?

MRS. ST. LOUIS: No, not yet. I just can't bring myself to go down there. My husband has spoken with him and he has gotten a lawyer. He said he looked scared.

MRS. PAUL: Good!

MRS. ST. LOUIS: Why do you say that?

MRS. PAUL: Because if he's scared, we still have a chance. He hasn't become so tough and bitter that he won't listen. I have a feeling that he might be ready to listen.

MRS. ST. LOUIS: Do you think so?

MRS. PAUL: Mrs. St. Louis, all I know is that these days even kids with good homes and good parents ignore all the warnings, get in with the wrong crowd, and get into trouble. I have learned to look for hope any place I can. Even the hardest shells may have cracks where a little light might get in. The fact that this is the first time your son has been arrested and the fact that he is scared may be one of those little cracks.

MRS. ST. LOUIS: What do you think I should do?

MRS. PAUL: Go see him. Talk to him. Tell him you love him and that you want him to come home.

MRS. ST. LOUIS: And you think that will accomplish something? I have told him that over and over again but he never listened.

MRS. PAUL: Maybe now he will. I hope now he will.

MRS. ST. LOUIS: (*Getting up to leave, holding out her hand*) No one is praying for that more than I am, Mrs. Paul. Thank you for listening. I'll let you know what happens.

MRS. PAUL: Please call me when you know something. And, Mrs. St. Louis...

MRS. ST. LOUIS: Yes?

MRS. PAUL: When you talk to Jimmy...

MRS. ST. LOUIS: Yes?

MRS. PAUL: ...remind him that he once wanted to be a veterinarian.

MRS. ST. LOUIS *smiles and closes the door behind her.*

Discussion

1. What would reminding Jimmy that he once wanted to be a veterinarian accomplish?

2. Do you consider Mrs. St. Louis a good parent? What more could she have done to keep her son out of trouble?

3. Why do you think Jimmy would rob people? Do you think that he really needs the money?

4. What role does peer pressure play in this situation?

5. Do you think that Jimmy will change after his experience in jail? Explain.

Another Friday Night

Topic
violence and sports

Characters
Cheerleaders for the Hillsdale High School varsity basketball team:
  Alison
  Wendi
  Cassie
  Sheryl
Miss Armstrong, their coach
Bus Driver

> *The scene takes place on a school bus in the parking lot of Green Mountain High School. It is 10:45 p.m., and Hillsdale has just won an important semi-final game against Green Mountain. Some Green Mountain fans have decided to take their anger out on the Hillsdale cheerleaders.*

MISS ARMSTRONG: *(Out of breath, concerned)* Is everyone here? Sheryl, count heads. We should have seventeen on the bus. Was any one hurt? I know the Green Mountain coach was calling the police, but I don't think they're here yet.

> *From outside of the bus comes vulgarity aimed at Hillsdale and the cheerleaders. Before the coach can stop her,* ALISON *has her head out of the bus window, shouting a reply.*

ALISON: (*Shouting*) Shove it! You are so brave now, it's a shame you couldn't show some of it on the court! Losers!

MISS ARMSTRONG: What are you doing? Alison, get in here, now! The situation is bad enough without you making it worse!

SHERYL: Miss Armstrong, I only count sixteen.

MISS ARMSTRONG: Count again.

SHERYL: (*Counting, then*) Sixteen.

MISS ARMSTRONG: Can we figure out who's missing? Is Cassie here?

CASSIE: Yup.

MISS ARMSTRONG: What about Wendi?

WENDI: I'm right here.

MISS ARMSTRONG: Where's Jennifer? I don't see Jennifer.

WENDI: She was in the girls' room when the fights broke out in the lobby. We all ran for the bus and I thought she was right behind us.

At that moment, a beer bottle slams against the side of the bus and shatters. No one is hurt, but the violence of the shattered bottle underscores the severity of the situation.

MISS ARMSTRONG: (*Preparing to leave the bus*) Under no circumstances are any of you to get out of this bus, do you understand?

ALISON: Where are you going?

MISS ARMSTRONG: To find Jennifer. The bus driver can lock the door behind me. Keep the windows closed and Alison, keep your mouth shut! All right?

ALISON: Ok, Miss Armstrong.

MISS ARMSTRONG: I'll be back in a minute.

MISS ARMSTRONG *leaves the bus and the door is locked behind her. The crowd is still noisy outside of the bus, but the police are nowhere in sight.*

BUS DRIVER: Is it always this bad?

CASSIE: Sometimes. The crowd can get pretty nasty.

BUS DRIVER: But this is only a high school basketball game!

CASSIE: Yeah, but it's Friday night, guys have been drinking, they want to show off in front of their girlfriends...

ALISON: And it was a big game, the semi-finals...

BUS DRIVER: But still, some of those kids were acting like animals. I saw one boy kicking this other guy in the face...over and over...animals...

WENDI: You should see what happens to them when they play at our school!

BUS DRIVER: Our students act this way too?

WENDI: A few of the jerks, after they've been drinking.

BUS DRIVER: Boys!

CASSIE: Hey, it's the girls too. A couple of those cheerleaders tonight had me by the hair and if I didn't punch one of them I would have been in trouble.

BUS DRIVER: It's just not right. You're children...

At that moment sirens are heard. The police arrive with an ambulance.

BUS DRIVER: Good, the police...

SHERYL: (*Concerned*) And an ambulance! Where's Jennifer and Miss Armstrong?

ALISON: Hey, guys, I'm getting real scared here. What if something happened to Jennifer?

WENDI: Don't worry, I'm sure... Here comes Miss Armstrong.

MISS ARMSTRONG comes back into the bus and closes the doors behind her. She is out of breath and upset. She is doing her best not to show the girls how upset she really is.

ALL: (*In a jumble*) Miss Armstrong, are you all right? Where's Jennifer? Is Jennifer all right? Why didn't you bring Jennifer back with you?

MISS ARMSTRONG: Calm down. Calm down. Now, listen to me. The bus driver is going to take you back to school. Your parents should be waiting for you. Please stay on the bus until your ride picks you up. Ok?

WENDI: Where's Jennifer?

SHERYL: What happened?

MISS ARMSTRONG: When I went back into the school I couldn't find her anywhere. I went to the locker room, the gym, the lobby. It was confusing because there were still a few fights going on. Then I remembered that Wendi said she went to the girls' room. When I ran over there, I saw a crowd around the door. My heart stopped. I saw the other coach and told her I was missing one of my girls. She asked if her name was Jennifer. It seems that several of the girls from Green Mountain found her alone in the bathroom, saw her cheerleading uniform and... She's in pretty bad shape. They called an ambulance.

ALISON: What did she say when you saw her?

MISS ARMSTRONG: She was still unconscious when I left. Listen, I've gotta get back there. I'm going to ride with her to the hospital. Will you girls be ok?

ALL: (*Upset*) Sure...

MISS ARMSTRONG: Ok, see you tomorrow.

MISS ARMSTRONG *tells the* BUS DRIVER *to get going, jumps off the bus, and runs toward the school. The girls watch her leave.*

ALISON: (*Trying to cheer things up*) Hey, guys, at least we won the game! (*No one answers her.*) No, I mean really, at least—

WENDI: Shut up, Alison, before I...

WENDI *stops herself, realizing that she is about threaten more violence. No one says anything else for the rest of the ride home.*

Discussion

1. Can girls be as violent as boys? Under what circumstances?

2. What do you think could make members of a crowd become violent at a sports event?

3. Do the cheerleaders on the bus do anything to provoke the trouble?

4. What could be done to calm people down in situations such as these?

5. Why does Wendi stop herself from completing her sentence?

Journal 12/22

Topic
weapons in school

Character
Teenager (male or female)

> TEENAGER *is writing in a marble notebook and*
> *speaking aloud.*

TEENAGER: Nobody touches me! Nobody! That's what
started this whole thing—that kid shoved
me. He did it on purpose, I know it, and he
got an attitude when I told him to keep his
hands to himself.

I wouldn't have pulled it on him if he
didn't start coming after me. I didn't want
nobody to get hurt— but you gotta protect
yourself.

He started coming at me and I pulled the
razor out of my pocket. He knew I was
serious. He knew I would have used it if I
had to. So, he stopped—cool, no trouble.

Then, this teacher starts running down the
hall. She was yelling, "Throw that knife
down! Throw it down, now!" She was a
gym teacher and she thought she was

tough. She came right up to me and put out her hand and said, "Give it to me!"

I don't know, there was something about the way she said it that kinda reminded me of my mother.

"Give it to me, now!" she shouted. She didn't ask me, she demanded—just like my mother does.

From that point on, everything moved so fast. All I remember is that I was thinking about my mother and this teacher went to grab the razor. I freaked. I remember yelling, "Don't touch me! Don't touch me!"

I guess I was waving the razor in front of me when I was yelling because they say that her hands got pretty cut up. All of a sudden somebody tackled me from behind. I think it was another kid. The razor flew out of my hand and everyone started yelling.

The police said that when they put me in the cop car, I was just staring straight ahead. "What kinda drugs are ya on, kid?" one of them said. "He's so messed up he can't even answer you," I heard another say.

I've been locked up for two days now. They said they called my mother, but she hasn't come down to the jail yet.

A lawyer showed up to talk to me this morning and I asked her when I could go home. She told me that she didn't know. She said it was a very serious offense. "But it's three days before Christmas," I said. "They gotta let me go home for Christmas."

"We'll see, Mr. Brooks," she said. "Well see." Then she left. "Hey, do me a favor," I called after her. "Tell that gym teacher that I'm real sorry and that I didn't mean to hurt her. Ok?"

"Sure, Pat."

"And tell my Mom..." but the lawyer was gone, "to have a merry Christmas."

Discussion

1. What triggers Pat's use of the razor? Why?

2. Can you explain why Pat is staring straight ahead as if s/he were dazed when s/he is put in the police car?

3. Why do you think that Pat's mother hasn't been to the jail yet?

4. With what crime should Pat Brooks be charged? What should the punishment be?

5. Why do you think the gym teacher reminds Pat of her/his mother?

The Evening News

Topic
weapons in school

Character
Newsperson

> NEWSPERSON *is sitting at an anchor desk reading the story into a television camera.*

NEWSPERSON: Police were called to Millbrook High School yesterday because a student reportedly stabbed a teacher with a knife. Janet Flynn, a gym teacher at the school, was hospitalized with wounds to her hands inflicted when she attempted to take a knife away from a student.

A spokesman for the school district said that there was an altercation between two students in the hallway. One student, fifteen-year-old Pat Brooks, pulled a knife, or a razor blade, from his pocket during the fight. Flynn, noticing trouble in the hall, ran to help. Upon seeing that Brooks had a weapon, she demanded that he put it down immediately. It was when Flynn attempted to take the weapon from the student that she was injured. In an ironic twist, it was another student who overpowered Brooks and who saved the teacher from further harm.

In an interview after the incident, Frank Raptis, the school principal, talked about the suspect. "I have known Pat Brooks since he was in ninth grade. Pat is a good student, but he does have a history of discipline problems. However, we have known for some time that he has a very difficult home life." Raptis declined to elaborate on any specific problems Brooks may have faced at home; however, several other people interviewed explained that there is a history of alcoholism and physical abuse in the Brooks home.

Ellen Quince, Brooks' social worker, was extremely upset about his arrest. "I have been working with Pat since he was seven years old. Just this year I got him to start keeping a journal. The little he let me read indicated to me that he was making real progress in terms of dealing with his problems at home. This is a tragedy, a real tragedy for everyone."

Even though Brooks is a minor, the District Attorney said that he was going to be tried as an adult on charges of attempted manslaughter.

Brooks is to remain in the Middlebrook County Jail until his arraignment because his family is unable to post bail.

Discussion

1. Why is the District Attorney going to try Pat Brooks as an adult? What does that mean for Pat? Do you think that it is fair that he be tried as an adult?

2. How could Pat have avoided all of this trouble?

3. Why was Pat's trouble predictable?

4. Should the charges against Pat be less severe because of his troubled family life?

Violence
at Home

Home

Topic
domestic violence

Characters
Three teenagers

> *Three teenagers stand in a straight line and face the audience. Even though they each speak separately, their delivery should give the impression that only one person is telling the story.*

1: He's usually

1, 2, 3: drunk.

2: He comes home late and starts screaming for something to eat.

3: "I want dinner!"

2: he yells.

1: He doesn't care that it's 1:30 in the morning.

3: "Get out of bed you lazy bitch!"

1: My mother gets out of bed.

3: She knows that things would only get worse if she ignored him.

1: "You better not be ignoring me again!"

1, 2, 3: Again.

3: My father has been beating my mother

1: for as long as I can remember.

2: When I was little, I just heard the

3: screaming.

1: As I got older,

2: I began to notice the

1: bruises.

3: "Get in this kitchen, now!"

2: My mother used to fight back.

1: She would never let him touch her.

3: She would always call the police.

1: "911. Is there an emergency?"

2: "Yes, my husband is here and he's drunk again. I'm afraid he is going to start hitting me and the children."

1: "What's the address?"

2: "234 Belvedere Court—555-1090—Greene."

3: "Get me some god damn dinner before I..."

1: "Is that him shouting in the background?"

2: "Yes, please hurry!"

1: "Just stay on the line, Ma'am. We have a patrol car in the vicinity. It will be there in three to four minutes. Just stay on the line..."

3: She must have called 911 a hundred times when I was growing up.

1: He must have hit her a hundred times when I was growing up.

1, 2, 3: "Mom, why don't you get out?

1: Why don't you

2, 3: leave him!"

1: She would tell us that it wasn't that easy and that when we grew up we would understand.

2: Well,

3: I'm in high school now,

1: and I still don't understand.

2: How could you stay with someone who beats you?

3: How could you stay with someone who beats your children?

2, 3: How could you?

1: "Where do you want me to go?"

3: she would say.

1: "Where do you want me to bring you kids? Any ideas? And what would we do for money?"

2: She has been with him now for over twenty years.

3: I'm surprised that he hasn't killed her.

2: I'm surprised that I haven't killed *him*.

1: I could, you know.

3: I really could.

2: Kill him, I mean.

1: After what he has put my mom through, he deserves

2: anything

3: he

1: gets. I know where to get a gun.

2: That would be easy.

3: One shot, right between the

1, 2, 3: eyes.

2: Or I could stab him or poison him or something.

1: Anything

3: to keep him away from my mother.

1: You don't know how many times I have dreamed of it.

2: But

3: one thing has always stopped me.

1: It's not that I'm afraid of getting caught.

2: Or of going to prison or anything.

3: No.

1: If I ever shot him,

2: or stabbed him,

3: or beat him like he beat us,

1: then I

2: would have turned out just

3: like

1: him.

2: And I would never want to give him that satisfaction.

Discussion

1. What are some causes of domestic violence?

2. Why do you think wives stay with their abusive husbands?

3. What can children who witness abuse do to help stop it?

4. Is domestic violence an isolated problem in society? Is it common? Explain.

5. Explain what the teenager means when s/he says, "I would never want to give him that satisfaction."

Journal 9/3

Topic
violence, abuse, and alcohol

Characters
Teenager (male or female)

> TEENAGER *writes in a marble notebook and speaks aloud.*

TEENAGER: I knew it. I knew she'd be drunk when I got home. I knew she would cause trouble like she always does. Why should the first day of school be any different?

She had that look in her eye—the look that says, "Go ahead, say something I don't like. Go ahead."

I walked into the house and she doesn't ask me a simple question like, "How was school today?" No. She looked at me and kinda smiled and said, "First day of school, huh? Did you screw up yet?"

I just looked at her. I didn't say anything. Nothing.

"I said did you screw up yet? Answer me!" she shouted as she walked over to me.

Now I could smell the reason why she was being so nasty. She was drunk again, and I started to get scared. I knew that if I didn't do something she was going to get crazy.

I said, "No Mom, not yet." And I started to go into my room. Real slow. No confrontations. I just wanted get away from her.

That's when she slammed me across the face.

She usually hits me with the back of her hand so that her wedding ring gets me. She always uses that ring.

I thought that things would calm down when school started. I thought that she would leave me alone for a while—like she did last year. She is always so mad at me. What did I do to her? I didn't make Dad die. Does she think that by hitting me she will bring him back? Does she think it will help anything?

Or does it just make her feel good?

Discussion

1. What do you think causes this mother to be violent?

2. What could this teenager do to prevent the abuse?

3. What role do you think alcohol plays in the mother's abusive behavior? What role to you think the death of the father plays?

4. Why could writing in a journal be beneficial to the teenager?

A Difference of Approach

Topic
parents who foster violence

Characters
Jeremy, a high school sophomore
Mr. Shea, Jeremy's father

> JEREMY *and* MR. SHEA *are at home when Jeremy's school calls.*

MR. SHEA: (*Answering the phone*) Hello. This is Mr. Shea. Yes...I see...No, he didn't tell me...He didn't?...Oh, that's good...Good...I will...Thank you, I will. (*Hangs up and turns to Jeremy*) So, what happened at school?

JEREMY: Nothing.

MR. SHEA: They just said you were in a fight.

JEREMY: Yeah. It was no big deal.

MR. SHEA: Who started it?

JEREMY: The other kid.

MR. SHEA: How did it start?

JEREMY: He was just being a jerk. We were taking this test in social studies and I wouldn't let him cheat off me. He got a 50 and I got a 97. He was pissed.

MR. SHEA: So what happened?

JEREMY: After class, in the hall, he started calling me names.

MR. SHEA: What sort of names?

JEREMY: You know, the ones they always call me... herb, scrub, punk.

MR. SHEA: Then?

JEREMY: Then he started shoving me against the lockers and saying he failed the test because of me. Some kids started to bunch up around us and then the principals came. They broke it up and brought us to the office.

MR. SHEA: And the other kid got five days out-of-school suspension for fighting?

JEREMY: Yeah.

MR. SHEA: And you didn't?

JEREMY: No.

MR. SHEA: (*Annoyed*) Why not? (JEREMY *doesn't answer. He knows the point his father is attempting to make and he doesn't want to play into his father's hand.* MR. SHEA *is getting more upset, and he raises his voice.*) Why not?

JEREMY: You know why not—because I didn't hit him back!

MR. SHEA: (*Now disgusted as well as annoyed*) How many times have I told you that if somebody hits you, you have to hit him back, harder? How many times? (*Waits for an answer but doesn't get one*) Are you going to let people push you around your whole life? Are you, Jeremy? (*Again, his son does not answer, and Mr. Shea softens a bit.*) Listen, son, you're a good kid. You're a top-notch student, but in today's world, that's not enough. You have to be able to take care of yourself!

JEREMY: I can take care of myself.

MR. SHEA: How? By letting someone bash your head into a locker?

JEREMY: I'm used to it.

MR. SHEA: That's not the point. The point is that you let him do it! The point is that if you let him get away with it once, he'll do it again, and again, and again! You have got to take care of the problem, Jeremy! You have got to hit the S.O.B. so hard that he won't pick on you again—that's the only solution!

JEREMY: I don't think that's the only solution.

MR. SHEA: What do you mean?

JEREMY: I don't think you always have to fight to solve everything.

MR. SHEA: It's a violent world, Jeremy, and it requires violent solutions. That's reality. (JEREMY *has heard this argument before but he doesn't know how to respond.* MR. SHEA *knows that he has not convinced his son, but, once again, he softens his attitude.*) Hey, listen, did he hurt you?

JEREMY: Not really. I might have a black eye coming up, though.

MR. SHEA: Let me see...Yeah, looks like you're gonna have a nice one. I'll get some ice for it.

JEREMY: No, Dad, it's ok, really, it's ok...

MR. SHEA: Sit still. I'm your father and I know what's best for you, right?

JEREMY: (*Reluctantly*) Yeah, Dad, sure...

MR. SHEA *gets up and walks toward the kitchen. When he is almost out of the room, he stops and turns to* JEREMY.

MR. SHEA: Hey, Jeremy, do me a favor?

JEREMY: What?

MR. SHEA: Next time you see that kid will you pop him in the face for me?

JEREMY: Just get me the ice, Dad, ok?

MR. SHEA: Ok, ok, I was just asking.

Discussion

1. How have the traditional father/son roles in this relationship been reversed?

2. Isn't the father correct when he says that it's a violent world? How could the son have argued this point?

3. How will other students react to Jeremy's refusal to fight? Should their reactions play a part in Jeremy's decision not to fight?

4. Should both Jeremy and the student who hit him be punished? Explain.

5. If you were the principal of a high school, what would you do to prevent fighting?

6. Should a parent encourage his or her child to fight? Explain.

The Two-Month-Old Quarterback

Topic
fostering passive or aggressive behavior in children

Characters
Mother
Father
Narrator

> *Each character stands separately on the stage. They face front and speak directly to the audience. Throughout the scene, MOTHER speaks to her imaginary daughter and FATHER speaks to his imaginary son. The scene opens in the nursery of a hospital.*

MOTHER: Oh, look, she's adorable!

FATHER: He's so big! Look at those hands!

MOTHER: She has such a sweet, little smile...

FATHER: He looks tough already...

NARRATOR: It starts very early. Right at birth, as a matter of fact—right in the hospital.

MOTHER: So delicate...

FATHER: What a bruiser...

MOTHER: Look at those long legs...those are the legs of a dancer...

FATHER: He's the first one in the second row...the one that looks like a linebacker...

NARRATOR: Some parents expect different things from their children. They expect "boy things" from boys and "girl things" from girls. In turn, without meaning to, they treat little girls differently from little boys.

MOTHER: You should see the nursery at home. We painted the room pink, of course, and I made beautiful lace curtains. She also has about a thousand teddy bears already! She is one lucky little girl.

FATHER: I know he's only a baby, but I don't want him to have all those stuffed dolls and animals. I don't want to start him off on the wrong foot, if you know what I mean. So, I bought him this little football—made of leather and everything. I think he's gonna be a quarterback.

NARRATOR: At first, the differences may be as basic as pink versus blue. But as children get older, the differences become more pronounced.

MOTHER: Come here and let me hug you, you little munchkin. Oh, you are so soft and cuddly. Mommy could just sit here all day and rock you in her arms.

FATHER: Stop kissing him all the time! Whenever I turn my back you have him in your lap hugging and kissing him like he was a little puppy!

NARRATOR: Girls should be soft. Boys should be tough. Girls should get hugs. Boys are meant to wrestle in the living room.

MOTHER: Honey, you don't want to buy that toy! You don't want a tool box. I know it's just like daddy's, but it's for boys. Why don't we get you another Barbie? Come over here to the doll section...

FATHER: Now, which one do you want, the sword that lights up and makes battle noises or the knife that squirts blood when you stab someone? I know. I wish you could get both too, but they're too expensive. Hey, what about these hand grenades?

NARRATOR: Sooner than most parents would like, their children become too old for toys. But even when all of the Barbies are packed away in the attic, parents still, inadvertently, teach their children many things.

MOTHER: Oh, honey, I'm so glad you picked the flute.

FATHER: What do you mean you want to play the clarinet?

MOTHER: Now you have to make a decision. Is it going to be tap or ballet? I'm sorry, but field hockey is *not* an option.

FATHER: We'll go to football camp in August. That way you'll be ready for the freshman team in the fall. What do you mean you want to play in the band? Would you rather be in the bleachers watching the game or on the field kicking the crap out of the other team? Come on now, get real!

NARRATOR: And when children become young adults, the lessons their parents teach them reach far beyond ballet or football.

MOTHER: I don't care if you think the teacher was wrong, I do not want you raising your voice in class for any reason. I want you to politely wait to be called on. There is nothing worse than a pushy woman, do you understand?

FATHER: I want you to hit him harder next time. To hell with this shoving him into a locker. If he starts with you I want you to hit him so hard that he'll never do it again, do you understand?

MOTHER: Brian's a nice boy. He's captain of the football team, honey. Now, I don't think that you could do better than that! So he yells at you sometimes; all boys do that. Your father has done it for years. Just tune him out. He'll get over it.

FATHER: So, you're taking Liddy Barker out tonight, huh? Nice girl, very nice girl. She can be a little pushy, though. You might have to remind her who wears the pants in the relationship.

NARRATOR: Sometimes those lessons are learned too well.

MOTHER: What do you mean that he slapped you? Let me see. Oh, honey, he did that? My god, why did you let him hit you? You have to stand up for yourself, Liddy. I won't always be here to get you out of trouble. Let me have the phone. I'm calling his father. Honey, go get some ice. They'll be lucky if I don't call the police!

FATHER: You did what? Why in the world did you hit the girl? That's no excuse! Your mother and I have been married for almost thirty years and I have never laid a hand on her, never! I raised you better than that, Brian.

NARRATOR: From the nursery through high school, parents instill values in their children every day.

MOTHER: (*On the phone*) Mr. Brown, this is Emily Barker...

NARRATOR: Oftentimes, without even knowing it.

MOTHER: ...Liddy's mother.

NARRATOR: Powerful, hidden messages are sent through hugs...

FATHER: (*On the phone*) Yes, I know...

NARRATOR: or the lack of hugs...

FATHER: I'm glad you called.

NARRATOR: ... or through "girl toys" versus "boy toys"...

MOTHER: Did your son tell you what happened?

NARRATOR: ...or through casual advice given before a date.

FATHER: Yes, yes, he did and I must apologize for his behavior.

MOTHER: What would make him do such a thing?

FATHER: I don't know. I just don't know...

NARRATOR: Unfortunately, some children learn these lessons all too well.

Discussion

1. How are the parents to blame for the actions of Liddy and Brian?

2. What in Liddy's past may have steered her toward becoming involved in an abusive relationship?

3. What in Brian's past may have made him abusive?

4. Describe the subtle messages both parents were sending to their young children. Explain how these messages could be considered sexist.

5. Is violent or abusive behavior determined by gender? Are these behaviors hereditary? Can they be taught?

6. What influences, other than their parents, may have helped to form Liddy and Brian's adult personalities?

7. Is it too late for Brian or Liddy to change his or her behavior? Explain.

Violent
Language

Laying Blame

Topic
violence and song lyrics

Characters
Senator Collins, chairman of the Committee on Youth and Violence
Audrey Styles, a teenager testifying before the committee
Greg Lamar, the mayor of a small city

> *The scene is Washington, DC. It is the final day of hearings for a congressional committee formed to investigate violence and young people. The last day's testimony concerns the effect violent songs have on young people. Mayor Lamar is finishing his statement as the scene begins.*

LAMAR: That is why, ladies and gentlemen, my city has proposed a ban on all music that contains violent messages against society, the police, or women. These songs are encouraging our young people to be violent. These songs encourage crime. These songs encourage sexual abuse. I defy any one of you to find one thing positive to say about the filth that some of these record companies produce. If our young people like to dance to this type of music, no problem. But we need to change the lyrics to something more socially acceptable. Songs are meant to be enjoyed; they are not meant to incite riots or encourage degenerate behavior. We already have parental advisory stickers on songs that contain explicit lyrics. Unfortunately, parents don't buy music; kids buy the music. Therefore, stickers for *parents* are ineffective. That is why the lawmakers in our city are working to pass a bill that would make it illegal to sell this type of music. I encourage you, here in Washington, to do the same thing on a national level. If we get rid of this music, we will get rid of an important link between violence and our young people. Thank you.

SENATOR: Thank you, Mr. Mayor. Our last guest today is Ms. Audrey Styles, a senior at The High School of Performing Arts in New York City. Ms. Styles.

AUDREY: Thank you, Senator Collins. You people just don't get it, do you? I mean, Mr. Mayor, it is all well and good that you are so concerned about the young people in your city, but you are way off base. Banning this music will not solve your problems. Banning this music will not stop the violence in society. You have it backwards. The violence in society has created this music. The poverty in this society has created this music. The desperation that young people feel today has created this music. It's like the old question, "Which came first, the chicken or the egg?" This music reflects what's going on in America and you are not going to solve anything with censorship and bans. You cannot make music that is socially acceptable when what is going on in cities all across this nation is not socially acceptable. I personally hate songs that are degrading to women. I deplore lyrics that incite violence. But, if you tell a kid that it is against the law to buy lyrics like that, what is the first thing that kid is going to do? He or she is going to try his or her hardest to get those lyrics. If you put special stickers on records that contain explicit language, those are going to be the first records to sell out at the record store. I won't even mention how such a ban as the one proposed by Mayor Lamar would infringe on our civil rights. To solve the problem of violence and young people in your city, Mr. Mayor, and across this country, we have to attack the cause of that violence. We have to attack poverty. We have to change the reality of the streets. Don't try to make song lyrics "socially acceptable." Make the lives of young people "socially acceptable" first. If we all focus on the cause, meaning poverty, rather than on the result, meaning music, I believe we will see these offensive lyrics disappear by themselves. Thank you.

SENATOR: Thank you, Ms. Styles.

Discussion

1. Do you think that music can encourage people to commit violent acts? To commit suicide? Has a song or piece of music ever made *you* feel more violent?

2. Do you think songs that encourage violence or contain vulgar lyrics should be banned?

3. If Audrey Styles "hates songs that are degrading," why do you think that she wouldn't support a ban on that type of music?

4. Could people who would agree with Ms. Styles and people who would agree with Mayor Lamar reach any compromise?

Respect

Topic
teachers and violent or abusive language

Characters
Mr. Hodges, a social studies teacher
Students in his class:
   Eric
   Martha
   J.D.
   Abby

> MR. HODGES *is standing in the hall, next to his room, between classes. He is attempting to get his students to class on time.*

MR. HODGES: *(Loudly, over the noise of the crowded hallway)* Let's go, let's go. You're gonna be late. Come on, Eric, if you don't get in this room right now, I'm gonna kick you in the pants so hard your butt will say "Size 10½". Move it, move it. *(Seeing a girl in his class kissing her boyfriend)* Abby, you are going to see him in about forty-five minutes. What do I have to do, drag you into class? Come on... *(The bell begins to ring.* MR. HODGES *moves into his room and addresses his class.)* All right, I want everybody to sit down and shut up! *(Shouting)* Shut up! (ERIC *is still talking.*) Eric, you better shut that mouth before I shut it for you, permanently, do

you understand? (ERIC *sits down and stops
talking.*) Smart boy...smart boy...

MARTHA: Mr. Hodges?

MR. HODGES: What?

MARTHA: Could you tell us what's on the test
tomorrow?

MR. HODGES: What are you, deaf? I told you that
yesterday. I'm not going to repeat myself.

MARTHA: I was absent yesterday, Mr. Hodges.

MR. HODGES: Too bad. Get it from one of your friends.
Now maybe you'll learn to come to school
instead of pretending you're sick every
other day.

MARTHA: Mr. Hodges, I really was—

MR. HODGES: (*Annoyed*) Enough noise. All women want
to do is talk, talk, talk—and spend money.
Right, guys? (*There is very little reaction from
the class. The girls ignore the comment and few
of the boys nod in agreement. The class
somehow knows that* MR. HODGES *really isn't
kidding around and they all sense his hostility.
They have learned to avoid most contact with
him.*) I said, "Right, guys?" What's the
matter with all you boys? Have your
girlfriends got you wrapped around their
little fingers? Is that it? (*Looking at* ABBY *and
remembering the scene in the hall prior to class*)
Do you have that boyfriend of yours
wrapped around your little finger, Abby?

ABBY: (*Not wanting the attention or a possible
problem*) Yeah, sure, Mr. Hodges, he's
wrapped around my little finger.

MR. HODGES: See, what did I tell you! You guys need to
exert yourselves. You need to slap a little
sense into those girlfriends of yours.

MARTHA: (*Finding the courage to confront him*) What did you say?

MR. HODGES: Just kidding, missy, just kidding. What's the matter, can't you take a little joke?

MARTHA: It's nothing to joke about, Mr. Hodges, and you know it. Nobody is "slapping" anything into me and nobody ever will.

MR. HODGES: Well, maybe if your Mommy or Daddy slapped your behind when you were younger you would have learned not to talk back to adults.

J.D.: (*Outraged*) What are you talking about? Listen to what you're saying!

MR. HODGES: (*Feeling threatened and lashing out with the authority of his position*) You stay out of this, mister, unless you want to find yourself going down to the office with pretty little Martha here.

MARTHA: (*Challenging him but not being disrespectful*) Why are you sending me down to the office? You are the one who was saying all the stuff about slapping sense into people. J.D.'s right. You should stop and listen to yourself for a minute. Sometimes you run this class like you were a storm trooper! "Get in here before I drag you in here" or "Sit down and shut up!" or "You should slap some sense into her!" I'm sorry, Mr. Hodges, but sometimes you are way out of line.

MR. HODGES: (*Seething with embarrassment and anger, he begins to bellow*) You are the only one that's out of line! How dare you talk to me like that!

MARTHA: How dare *you* talk to us the way you do!

MR. HODGES: I will not stand here and allow you to undermine my authority in front of this class. Who do you think you are? I am the teacher. You are the student. And, I might add, you are going to be a very sorry student when I finish with you. Get out. Take your books and get out of my classroom. (MARTHA *gathers her things quietly and leaves the room. The class is stunned at what just happened.* MR. HODGES *slams the door to his room and turns to the class.*) Does anyone else have anything to say?...I didn't think so. You young people must learn how to talk to those in authority like your parents, other adults, your teachers. You must also learn how to talk to each other! I stand in the hall between classes and I can't believe the language I hear! It's revolting. If I hear the "F" word once, I hear it a thousand times a day! And from young ladies, too! You never hear me use vulgarity! Young people today need a good lesson in speaking properly, in speaking politely, in speaking with respect! Now, take out your textbooks and read chapter twenty-seven! I'm giving you a quiz on it at the end of the period. (*The class groans at the thought of a pop quiz.*) And keep your mouths shut! I want quiet in this room for the next thirty minutes. Get to work.

Discussion

1. Even though he uses no vulgarity, how is Mr. Hodges' language abusive?

2. Name a few of the inappropriate things Mr. Hodges says. Explain why you think that they are inappropriate.

3. Was Martha wrong to confront Mr. Hodges? Explain. What else could she have done?

4. How would you react to Mr. Hodges if he were your teacher? Explain what you would do if you were bothered by his language.

Show Time[*]

Topic
violence and song lyrics

Characters
Rapacious, a popular rap artist
Melody, his girlfriend

RAPACIOUS *is struggling with the lyrics of a new song. He is in the process of searching for new and different rhymes when his girlfriend interrupts him.* RAPACIOUS *is at a desk, talking to himself, when the scene begins.*

RAPACIOUS: (*Attempting to say the lines in rhythm*)

Hey, babe, I'm wantin somethin' more,
But every time I look at you you're lookin'
   like a ...

No, no, no. How may times can I say "whore" in a song? It's even getting boring to me! Let's see...

Hey, honey, let me scratch your itch.
I really, really love you and I want you
   for my...

(*Frustrated and annoyed with himself*) "Bitch," "bitch," every other word is "bitch." I can't

---

[*] This scene contains offensive language.

think any more. I can't write any more! (*Melodramatically*) My career as an artist is over!

RAPACIOUS *slams down his pencil when* MELODY *enters. She sees his outburst and goes to comfort him.*

MELODY: (*Giving him a hug*) What's the matter, baby, you got writer's block again?

RAPACIOUS: Ah, I just can't hack it any more.

MELODY: Can't hack what, honey?

RAPACIOUS: Writing this stuff. The only songs that sell have "bitch" and "'ho" in every other line. I just can't write it anymore.

MELODY: You know, I was meaning to talk to you about that.

RAPACIOUS: About what?

MELODY: About all that "beatin' on bitches" and "killin all the cops" and "you a ho—me a ho" stuff. Honey, it's startin' to get to me. Sometimes I wonder what you think of me or that you really want to call me a bitch or a whore or something.

RAPACIOUS: Hey, I never called you names like that. Never.

MELODY: You're damn right you didn't. You knew better. I would never stand for it. But why are you always putting it in your songs?

RAPACIOUS: Like I said before, because that's what sells.

MELODY: You think that kids won't buy your music if you don't write that stuff?

RAPACIOUS: That's what my producer says.

MELODY: Have you ever tried to get him to put out one of those beautiful love songs that you used to sing to me when we first started going out?

RAPACIOUS: *She* doesn't want to hear that kind of stuff. And neither do the kids.

MELODY: Your producer is a woman?

RAPACIOUS: Yup.

MELODY: I never knew that.

RAPACIOUS: Well, now you do. Anyway, it doesn't make any difference. Look at all the people who are on top in this industry. Listen to their songs. Almost all of them are making money with the "bitch" and "whore" stuff.

MELODY: I wonder what the women in their lives are like? I wonder how they can stand being talked about like that. It's demeaning, degrading, and disgusting. And, honey, I want you to be different.

RAPACIOUS: That's easy to say, but it's a lot more difficult to try to *sell*. And the first person we gotta sell is my producer.

MELODY: Call her up!

RAPACIOUS: What?

MELODY: Right now. Give me the phone. I'll dial. I've got an idea.

RAPACIOUS: (*Reluctantly handing Melody the phone*) Wait a minute. What are you going to say?

MELODY: I'm not going to say anything. And neither are you.

RAPACIOUS: Melody, what are you talking about?

MELODY: What was the name of that sweet thing you sang real soft to me on our first date?

RAPACIOUS: It doesn't have a name yet.

MELODY: Well, when I get Miss Producer on the line, I want you to sing it to her just like you sang it to me that night.

RAPACIOUS: Do you think she'll go for it?

MELODY: It's worth a shot.

RAPACIOUS: But it doesn't have any "bitches" in it.

MELODY: Exactly! I'm dialing now, honey. It's showtime!

Discussion

1. Were you surprised that Rapacious' producer is a woman?

2. Why do you think that songs with vulgar lyrics are so popular?

3. Which are worse: songs with violent lyrics or songs with vulgar lyrics? Explain.

4. Explain Rapacious' professional dilemma. What would you do in his situation?

"Word, Words, Words"

Topic
using language that avoids conflict

Characters
Three teenagers:
  1 - Narrator
  2 - Negative Expressions
  3 - Positive Expressions

> *The three teenagers stand and face the audience.*

1: Did you know that the words or expressions you use will determine how people respond to you? Like teachers who say...

2: "This student is lazy, uncooperative and cheats!"

1: Try a "softer" approach.

3: "This student can do more when he tries, should learn to work with others, and, unfortunately, depends upon others to do his work."

1: You are saying the same thing but with language that is not as confrontational. It is not so "hard." There are parents who say...

2: "Compared to your sister, your grades are rotten!"

3: "I know that you are working at your own level."

1: Or

2: "Your little boy stole my son's shovel."

3: "Your little boy took my son's shovel without permission."

1: Hey, in both cases you get the shovel back, but if you use less confrontational language, you may also get an apology.

2: "Stole? My son doesn't steal!"

3: "Oh, I'm sorry, I didn't realize the shovel was yours."

1: The same holds true when parents speak to teenagers and when teenagers speak to their parents. Less confrontational language helps to avoid a fight.

2: "That boyfriend of yours is rude!"

3: "You know, Bob is outspoken at times."

1: "Rude" versus "outspoken." Their definitions are similar but their connotations are worlds apart.

2: "You're lying, Mom!"

3: "Mom, I think you are stretching the truth a little bit."

1: Or

2: "Why are you always sitting around watching TV and wasting your time?"

3: "Don't you think you could make better use of your weekends?"

1: The point is not to lie, or to skirt the truth, or to avoid confronting a problem. If your boyfriend is always lying, you need to tell him. But you can do it in a way that won't cause more problems. We all have to listen carefully to the words we choose and decide if they are making things better or making them worse.

2: Bored.

3: Not challenged.

2: Dope.

3: Capable of doing better.

2: Sloppy.

3: Could be neater.

2: Mean.

3: Having difficulty getting along with others.

2: Time and time again.

3: Usually.

2: Clumsy.

3: Not well coordinated.

2: Selfish.

3: Doesn't share.

2: Bashful.

3: Reserved.

1: We have to say what we mean...

2: ...but we also have to listen to what we are saying.

3: Don't let negative, confrontational expressions...

2: ...cause more problems...

1: ...than you already have.

Discussion

1. The denotation of a word is that word's specific meaning (e.g., "bread" is a food). The connotation of a word is its suggested meaning, which is different from its specific meaning (e.g., "bread" can also be used as a dated, slang term for "money"). Discuss the denotative meaning and the connotative meanings of the following words: cool; sloppy; delinquent.

2. Name other words whose connotative definitions differ from their denotative definitions.

3. If you use less confrontational language, are you "skirting the truth?" Is there ever a time when you should use confrontational language?

4. What is the difference between forceful language and confrontational language?

5. Describe a few situations where words could be used as "weapons."

Parting Words*

Topic
vulgar language

Characters
Mr. Mars, a biology teacher
Freshmen in his class:
    Jessica
    Beth

> MR. MARS *is reviewing for an important unit test. However,* JESSICA *has more important things she needs to discuss with* BETH.

MR. MARS: (*Lecturing at the board*) Finally, you need to be able to distinguish between the actual nerve ending and the synapses between the nerves. (*Noticing that* JESSICA *is talking to* BETH, *he directs his comment to them.*) Girls, this is important stuff I'm reviewing.

BETH: Sorry, Mr. Mars. (*Turns around in her seat and stops talking*)

MR. MARS: Ok, now, I am also going to ask you to label the various parts of the nerve itself. I will have a diagram and— (JESSICA *begins to talk again*) Jessica, come on, turn around. (*Still in a non-threatening tone*) You are starting to

---

* This scene contains offensive language.

get on *my* nerves now! The test is tomorrow. I'm sure what you have to tell Beth can wait until after class.

JESSICA: (*Reluctantly turning around and with an attitude*) It can't.

MR. MARS: Sorry, but it's going to have to. All right, if you all look at the back of chapter nine, you will see a diagram of the entire nervous system. I want you to focus on— (JESSICA *has started talking to* BETH *again.* BETH *realizes that* MR. MARS *is getting angry, but she doesn't know how to make* JESSICA *be quiet. For the first time,* MR. MARS *speaks sternly.*) Jessica, this is the third time I've asked you to stop talking. I am not going to ask you again. Either you turn around and pay attention or go down to the office. I refuse to continue to allow you to disrupt this class.

JESSICA *once again reluctantly turns around but this time she mutters loud enough for the class and* MR. MARS *to hear her.*

JESSICA: He's such an asshole.

MR. MARS: (*Responding to the comment*) All right, Jessica, out.

JESSICA: (*Packing up her books loudly, getting ready to leave for the office*) Gladly.

MR. MARS: (*As* JESSICA *is walking to the door, he begins to write a discipline referral.*) Is there anything else you would like to say about me or about the class before you leave us today?

JESSICA: (*Standing in the door*) Yeah. Fuck you!

JESSICA *slams the door. The class doesn't know how to react. Everyone is quiet and looking at* MR. MARS *to see what he is going to do. Initially, he is startled by the vulgarity. But he quickly regains his composure.*

MR. MARS: (*Responding to what* JESSICA *said*) Well, I guess she about summed it up. Now, let's get back to the review before the class is over.

Discussion

1. Was Mr. Mars "out of line" in the way he treated Jessica in class?

2. What do you think caused Jessica to use such vulgar language?

3. How do you think the principal should deal with Jessica's vulgarity?

4. Had you been Mr. Mars, how would you have responded to Jessica?

5. Is it common for students to speak to teachers that way? Is it common for students to speak to each other that way? What's the difference?

Violence
& Dating

"It's Ok, really..."

Topic
violence and dating

Characters
Two seniors who have been going out for more than a year:
   Al
   Missy
Patty, Missy's friend

> *It is after school and* AL *and* MISSY *are at the top of a stairwell on the second floor of the high school.* AL *has* MISSY *pressed into a corner and they are obviously having a heated discussion.* MISSY *looks uncomfortable and is trying to get away.* AL *keeps her in the corner as he talks.*

AL: What do you mean you think we are having problems?

MISSY: I don't know, Al. It's just that...

AL: Don't you think we should go out any more?

MISSY: I don't know, Al. Would you let go of my arm? You're hurting me.

> AL *lets go of* MISSY's *arm but keeps her in the corner.*

AL: Missy, I love you, don't you know that?

MISSY: I know, Al. I love you too. It's just that I think we have to work a few things out, that's all.

AL: Like what? We've been going out for over a year. I thought everything was great!

MISSY: That's part of the problem. When everything is going the way *you* want it, things are great! When we do what you want to do, things are great! Whenever I say that I don't want to do something, you get crazy!

AL: (*Raising his voice again*) We always do what you want to do. Don't we always take your little sister along with us to the beach? Don't we always go to see those dumb movies that you want to see? Don't we? (*Grabbing her arm again*) Don't we?

MISSY: Al, you're hurting me again.

Just as AL *grabs* MISSY's *arm,* PATTY *walks into the stairwell. He lets go just in time to avoid detection.*

PATTY: Hey, guys! What're ya doing?

MISSY: (*Covering up her emotions as well as possible*) Hey, Patty. Nothing. We were just talking.

PATTY: (*Seeing that* MISSY *is upset, she takes a step toward her*) Hey, Missy, are you Ok?

MISSY: Yeah, I'm fine.

AL *looks away, annoyed at the interruption.*

PATTY: (*Still sensing trouble*) Is there anything I can do?

MISSY: (*With urgency in her voice, not wanting* PATTY *to provoke* AL *any further*) No, no. It's Ok, really...I'll call you later.

PATTY: Ok. Later.

> PATTY *leaves reluctantly.* MISSY *waits for her to go before saying anything, but* AL *makes the first move. As soon as he sees that* PATTY *is gone, he slaps* MISSY *across the face as hard as he can.* MISSY *brings her hands to her face, but* AL *pulls her hair so that he can look her in the eye.*

AL: *(With uncontrolled anger)* I thought I told you I didn't want you speaking to that nosy bitch!

MISSY: *(Crying, not knowing what to say or do to keep him from hitting her again)* Al, please, I didn't mean anything by it. She's my friend. I'm sorry...I forgot that you said...

AL: Shut up! (AL *moves to hit* MISSY *again. This time* MISSY *wrenches free and begins to run down the hall.* AL *doesn't run after her. But, following a pattern familiar to* MISSY, *he calls after her.)* Missy, stop. I'm sorry. I just want to talk...Missy, please. I love you...Missy...

Discussion

1. Why do you think Missy doesn't want Patty to know she is having a problem with Al?

2. If Al loves Missy, why do you think he abuses her?

3. Why has Missy stayed with Al for over a year if the relationship is abusive?

4. Could Patty have been more help to Missy? Explain.

5. What would you have done if you were in Patty's position?

6. What steps could Missy take to stop the abuse?

7. What did you feel as you listened to Al talk to Missy?

The Health Class #1

Topic
defining abusive relationships

Characters
Mr. D., a health teacher
Ellen Michaels, a counselor
Rob
James
Grace
Ann
Karen

> MR. D *is concluding his class study of violence in society. Several students are sitting in desks listening.*

MR. D.: To wind up our unit on violence, I thought it would be interesting to invite a counselor from the Counseling Center to talk to you about her experiences with violence, teenagers, and relationships. Ellen, do you want to come up?

> ELLEN MICHAELS *gets up from one of the student desks and comes to the front of the class.*

ELLEN: Hi, everyone. I'm told that you guys have gone over all of the background information about rape, date rape, and abuse. What I want to do today is to put a "face" on all the violence we hear about between couples in high school. Stop me whenever you have a comment or if I've said something you don't understand.

ROB: (*With an attitude*) Wait a minute. Right off—what do you mean "put a face on violence"?

ELLEN: Good. What I mean is that I want to make violence in relationships real for you. I want to help you see the people behind the numbers.

GRACE: Numbers? What numbers?

ELLEN: Ok, let's talk numbers for a minute. (*Writes "28%" on the board*) Number: Twenty-eight percent of dating teens are involved in intimate violence. (*Writes "20%" on the board*) Number: Twenty percent of female homicide victims are between fifteen and twenty-four years of age. Many die as a result of conflicts with boyfriends. (*Writes "61%" on the board*) Number: Sixty-one percent of rape cases take place before the victim is eighteen years old. (*She pauses to let the numbers sink in*) These are some of the numbers. But what do they mean? To get an even clearer picture, can anyone give me some words to describe victims of abuse?

ANN: What about "female"?

ELLEN: Right. Many times the victims are women and the aggressors are men.

ROB: (*Interrupting*) Yeah, well the girls are guilty too, you know.

ELLEN: What do you mean?

ROB: I mean they ask for it. They flirt with other guys, they wear tight skirts, they—

KAREN: Wait a minute! I can't believe you just said "girls ask for it!"

ROB: They do!

KAREN: That is the stupidest thing I've ever heard! Do you really think a girl wants to be slapped around by her boyfriend?

ANN: Or that a girl wants to be raped? Be serious.

ROB: I am serious. I don't think that it's always the boy's fault. (*To* ELLEN) Is it?

ELLEN: There is never any reason or excuse for violent behavior. It's wrong. Period. But in our society, boys are almost expected by their peers to be aggressive to their girlfriends or to be controlling. Some boys think that being aggressive or domineering is the right way to behave in a relationship. It isn't and that's the problem.

ANN: Does being jealous have anything to do with it? My boyfriend is really jealous all the time.

ELLEN: Absolutely! Extreme jealousy is sometimes thought of as a sign of love. But it's not!

JAMES: What about when a girl is jealous of you?

ELLEN: Same thing. You have to realize that jealous behavior can lead to abuse in a relationship. Now, can you think of any other words that may describe someone who is the victim of violence in a relationship?

GRACE: What about "depressed"?

ELLEN: Good.

JAMES: "Nervous."

ELLEN: Right.

ANN: I know a girl whose boyfriend used to hit her and all she would do was stay by herself all the time.

ELLEN: Yes, many times victims of abusive relationships isolate themselves from family and friends.

MR. D.: Ellen, you have about three minutes until the bell.

ELLEN: Ok, I see I'm going to have to come back. But let's quickly go over what we have accomplished so far today. We talked about some statistics concerning victims of abusive relationships, and we described the behavior of people who are victims. Next time, I want to pinpoint abusive acts and discuss what we can do both as victims and as friends of victims to stop abusive behavior. I also want you to do me a favor. When I come back, I want you to switch sex roles.

ROB: Hey, what? I ain't switching nothing!

ELLEN: What I mean is, guys, I want you to look at relationships from a girl's point of view. And girls, I want you to see things from a guy's point of view. Write down some of your observations.

GRACE: Do we have to? I mean (*looking at* JAMES) I would rather not sink that low.

JAMES: Hey, that goes for me too, sweetheart!

GRACE: Sweetheart?

ELLEN: (*Interceding*) Calm down. Calm down. I didn't mean to start a war here.

ROB: But—

ELLEN: (*Interrupting*) Try.

The bell rings to end the period. The class begins to leave.

ELLEN: Just try it. See you next time.

Discussion

1. What are some of the reasons relationships may become abusive?

2. Do you know anyone involved in an abusive relationship? Who is the abuser? Who is the victim? What usually causes the abuse to take place? Is there anything you can do, as an observer, to help the situation?

3. Which people are in the best position to help teenagers who find themselves in abusive relationships? Parents? Teachers? Friends? Counselors? Why?

The Health Class #2

Topic
staying in abusive relationships

Characters
Mr. D., a health teacher
Ellen Michaels, a counselor
Rob
James
Grace
Ann
Karen

> *This is the second part of* ELLEN MICHAELS' *visit to*
> MR. D.'s *class, in which she is talking to the students*
> *about violence in adolescent relationships. Several*
> *students are sitting in desks, listening.*

MR. D.: I'm sure you all remember our class last week with Ellen Michaels from the Counseling Center.

ROB: Yeah—what a class! She wants us to act like girls!

MR. D.: What she wanted was for all of you to try to expand your narrow fields of vision to see certain situations from other perspectives—especially when it comes to teenagers, dating, and violence.

ROB: That's what I said—think like a girl.

ANN: Hey, Rob, that really wouldn't be all that bad, would it?

ROB: No comment.

MR. D.: As I told you yesterday, Ellen has agreed to come back today and finish the discussion we began last week. She should be here any minute.

ELLEN *comes hurrying in.*

ELLEN: Sorry I'm late.

ROB: (*Under his breath*) Just like a woman.

ELLEN: (*Hearing the comment*) The first thing we are going to do today is abolish all sexist comments. (*Glancing at* ROB)

ROB: Sorry.

ANN: (*To* ROB) Just like a guy!

ELLEN: (*To* ANN) From everyone!

ANN: Ok.

ELLEN: Last week we went over some statistics about violence and young people. Today, I want to touch on some reasons *why* people stay in violent relationships and some ways we can help people who are victims of abuse.

GRACE: (*Raising her hand*) What exactly do you mean by "abuse?" Are you just talking about girls getting beat up by their boyfriends?

ELLEN: That's a good question. Of course physical violence constitutes abuse, but I'm also talking about threats, coercion, intimidation, and extreme jealousy.

GRACE: You know, whenever my boyfriend and I have a fight, he drives like a maniac—on purpose!

ELLEN: That's intimidation—and it's abusive!

JAMES: My girlfriend is always accusing me of looking at other girls. She is so jealous I can't believe it! I can't even talk to girls in my class about homework without her getting crazy.

ELLEN: Extreme jealousy can be a form of abuse, too, if your girlfriend is trying to exert control with it.

ROB: Why would anybody stay in a relationship like that? I would have gotten out of there fast!

ELLEN: That brings us to another point. Why do people stay in abusive relationships? (*Asking class*) Any ideas?

GRACE: They're afraid.

ELLEN: Afraid of what?

ANN: Afraid of being alone or of not finding another boyfriend.

ELLEN: Right. Why else?

JAMES: Maybe they think they can change the person.

ELLEN: What do you mean?

JAMES: Like, say this guy smacks his girlfriend around but she still really likes him so she keeps hanging around with him, hoping to get him to stop hitting her.

ELLEN: Excellent! Anything else?

GRACE: I know this girl who always says her boyfriend doesn't hit her but I know he really does.

ELLEN: That's called "denial." She is denying the fact that she is being abused. I see that Mr. D. is signaling that we are running short of time again. This has been another great discussion. We've gone over a lot of definitions and facts and statistics, but I really want to leave you with more. Let's try something.

ROB: Oh, no. You are not going to ask us to think like girls now, are you?

ELLEN: No.

GRACE: Don't start again, Rob.

ELLEN: I want you all to write down one way you could help a good friend who is in an abusive relationship.

JAMES: You mean ways to break off the relationship?

ELLEN: I mean any suggestion that would help stop the abuse.

The class begins to think and write.

JAMES: (*After a minute*) That's easy. If a guy slugs you, slug him back.

ELLEN: That sounds like one solution, but violence really can't be an answer.

ANN: What about just being there to listen?

ELLEN: Good. Being a supportive and non-judgmental friend is the first step in helping.

ROB: What about talking to the friends of other people you know in the same situation and asking them to explain how they handled it?

ELLEN: Yes. It's important that the person who is being abused knows that he or she is not alone—that there are many teenagers who experience abuse in a relationship.

KAREN: Tell the friend that he or she doesn't deserve to be treated so badly.

ELLEN: You do that by building up their self-esteem. Good. That will help the person to stay out of abusive relationships in the future.

JAMES: Hey, what about calling the cops?

Everyone laughs.

ELLEN: Not so fast, not so fast. Abuse is a crime. The victims need protection. Calling the police is not a bad idea.

MR. D.: Ellen, two minutes till the bell.

ELLEN: Ok, Ok. Listen, abuse in relationships is happening. It's happening to kids like you every day. Even though the abuse itself is wrong and dangerous, what is more outrageous is to do nothing about it. If you are in an abusive relationship, tell someone. If you see someone you care about in an abusive relationship, tell someone. Because to keep quiet about it may be just as dangerous as the abuse itself. (*The bell rings to end the period. The class begins to leave.*) Thanks, everyone.

MR. D.: Thanks, Ellen.

Discussion

1. Other than physical violence, list some ways a relationship may be abusive.

2. What is the benefit of seeing situations from another perspective (for example, for a guy to see a relationship from his girlfriend's perspective)?

3. Name some reasons why people stay in abusive relationships.

4. What can you do to help someone get out of an abusive relationship?

5. Do you think that abuse is a problem in any of the relationships you have observed? Explain.

6. Define the following terms and explain what role they have in an abusive relationship: coercion; intimidation; denial; self-esteem.

The Ride Home

Topic
violence and dating

Characters
Anna, Paulie's girlfriend
Lisa, Anna's friend
Jenny, another student
Mrs. McAdam, a high school teacher

>ANNA *and* LISA *stand in the hallway outside of* JENNY's *math class. They have both gotten bathroom passes and have met to discuss how to handle* ANNA's *"problem."*

LISA: Are you sure she has math this period?

ANNA: Yeah, that's what Mitchell told me yesterday. She is supposed to be in Sequential One. Room 309.

>LISA *and* ANNA *walk by room 309 and surreptitiously look for* JENNY.

LISA: Did you see her?

ANNA: Yeah, she was sitting in the first row over by the window.

LISA: Well, what do you want to do?

ANNA: I'm gonna get her.

LISA: Now? You mean just walk into the class and start with her?

ANNA: No. We're going to wait for the bell to ring and I'll get her in the hall.

LISA: Anna, don't you think that you should at least wait until after school? You're going to get caught and they'll give you five days of out-of-school suspension.

ANNA: I don't care what they give me. I gotta teach this bitch not to mess around with my boyfriend!

LISA: Are you even sure it was her?

ANNA: Mitchell wouldn't lie to me. He's going out with my cousin. He said he saw Jenny in Paulie's car last Friday night. That's all I gotta know. How long 'til the bell?

LISA: About a minute or so. What are you going to do?

ANNA: When she comes out of class, I want you to get on one side of her and I'll get on the other. She won't be able to run. Then, I'll ask her a few questions.

LISA: And if you don't like the answers?

ANNA: And if I don't like the answers, I'll rip her hair out! (*Both girls laugh. The bell to end class rings.*) That's the bell. Get on the other side of the door. (LISA *moves to the other side of the door. Students come out of the math class.* JENNY *finally comes out, too.* LISA *slips behind her and* ANNA *confronts her. Sounding as tough as she can, she shoves* JENNY'*s shoulder to make her stop.*) Wait a minute. I want to talk to you.

JENNY: (*Surprised but not yet feeling threatened*) Oh, hi Anna. (*Seeing* LISA) Hi, Lisa.

ANNA: Were you in Paulie's car last Friday night?

JENNY: What?

ANNA: I said, were you and Paulie driving around in his car Friday night?

JENNY now realizes that ANNA means to start trouble and begins to get frightened. A crowd of students begins to form around them in the hallway.

JENNY: Last Friday? No, no, I was grounded last Friday night. My mom caught me...

LISA: (*Interrupting*) She didn't say last Friday night. She said this Friday night.

JENNY: This Friday? Ah, I don't remember.

ANNA: Well you better remember fast because I'm about to beat your face in.

JENNY: (*Now really scared*) Listen, Anna, Paulie gave me and my sister a ride home from the mall Friday night. It was no big deal. We met him while we were waiting for the bus and he said, "Why don't you guys let me give you a ride home?" That was it. I swear.

ANNA: That was it?

JENNY: Yeah, I swear.

MRS. McADAM, an English teacher, is now trying to work herself through the crowd to get to the two girls. She reaches them just as ANNA is about to lose it.

MRS. McADAM: Hey, hey, what's going on here?

ANNA: (*Realizing that if she wants to do anything to JENNY she has got to move fast.*) You're lying!

ANNA lunges for JENNY. JENNY ducks and MRS. McADAM restrains ANNA.

MRS. McADAM: (*To* ANNA) You! Calm down! You both are about five seconds away from out-of-school suspension.

ANNA: But...

MRS. McADAM: No "buts!" I'm getting sick of the way students at this school deal with their problems. When are you all going to realize that you can't solve your problems by fighting? (*The girls, including* ANNA, *have calmed down and begun to listen to* MRS. McADAM) Now, instead of me having to drag the both of you all the way down to the office, do you want to come into my room and talk? I don't promise any miracles, but I will promise you a "safe zone" where you can both discuss this. What do you say? Jenny?

JENNY: Ok.

MRS. McADAM: Anna?

ANNA: But she...

MRS. McADAM: No "buts," Anna, remember?

ANNA: All right.

They all begin to move into MRS. McADAM's *room.*

MRS. McADAM: Come on, we have some work to do.

Discussion

1. Does Anna have a problem with Jenny or is her problem with herself? Explain.

2. Do you think the two girls can settle their problems simply by talking about them with Mrs. McAdam?

3. Define "mediation." How could mediation play an important part in keeping the peace between Anna and Jenny?

Paulie's Story

Topic
violence and dating

Characters
Paulie, Anna's boyfriend
Mark, Paulie's friend

> PAULIE *is in the cafeteria having lunch.* MARK *hurries in to tell him some important news.*

MARK: Paulie, did ya hear?

PAULIE: Did I hear what?

MARK: Did you hear about Anna?

PAULIE: Oh, not again. What did she do this time?

MARK: Well, I heard that she cornered Jenny Phillips in the hall last period and was about to rearrange her face.

PAULIE: Why?

MARK: Anna was yelling something about seeing Jenny in your car Friday.

PAULIE: I can't believe it. Do you know why she's upset? I was at the mall last Friday and when I was leaving I saw Jenny and her sister waiting for a bus. So I offered them a ride home They took it. That's it! End of story.

MARK: Did you tell Anna?

PAULIE: No. It was no big deal. Anyway, I knew that she would just get all jealous over nothing.

MARK: Well, someone told her and she flipped out. I can't believe that she would get so crazy over a little ride home from the mall.

PAULIE: Well, you don't know Anna. She is unbelievably jealous. All the time. She is always asking me where I went, who I went with, and if there were any other girls around.

MARK: It sounds like she doesn't trust you. Have you ever messed around on her or anything?

PAULIE: Never! If I even looked at another girl Anna would kill me.

MARK: Then why is she so jealous?

PAULIE: I have no idea. It's like she's trying to tell me what to do all the time—where to go, who to talk to, who *not* to talk to.

MARK: It sounds like it goes way beyond jealous. She sounds like a control freak to me.

PAULIE: What do you mean?

MARK: Do you remember when we had that guest speaker in Health?

PAULIE: That woman from the counseling center who was talking about violence and dating?

MARK: Yeah.

PAULIE: Listen, Mark, I never hit Anna, ever.

MARK: That's not what I mean. She said that jealousy could develop into a form of abuse—that people who were too jealous of their boyfriend or girlfriend were just trying to control them.

PAULIE: Yeah, right. Do you think that's what Anna is trying to do to me?

MARK: Well, you said that she is always asking you where you went or who you were speaking to. She sounds like she's your mother more than your girlfriend.

PAULIE: Ok, smart guy, then how does that explain why Anna wanted to wipe the floor with Jenny? That has nothing to do with controlling *me*.

MARK: No, it doesn't have anything to do with you. It's Anna. Maybe she thinks that she's not good enough for you or something. Maybe she thinks that she has to knock all the other girls out of competition so that you will only think of her. Maybe she has a problem with...What's that called?

PAULIE: Self-esteem.

MARK: Yeah, self-esteem. Maybe she's being really jealous and controlling because she has a low opinion of herself.

PAULIE: This is getting too confusing.

MARK: All I know is that Anna is in Mrs. McAdam's room right now trying to work things out with Jenny.

PAULIE: I hope McAdam is keeping them on separate sides of the room. Do you think I should go see what's happening?

MARK: Yeah.

PAULIE: Do you think I should bring up all this self-esteem stuff?

MARK: Not at first. Anna's still pretty worked up. She might take a swing at you.

PAULIE: Yeah, I'll just go and try to calm her down. Then, in a couple of days...or a week...

MARK: Or a month...

PAULIE: I'll say something to her.

MARK: Good.

PAULIE: (*Getting up to leave*) See you later, Mark...and thanks.

MARK: No problem. Good luck, Paulie. And remember, if things get tough, duck!

Discussion

1. Explain how jealousy could be a way to control a person. Explain how this type of situation could become abusive.

2. Define "self-esteem." How could low self-esteem be a cause of jealousy?

3. Why do you think that Anna didn't speak to Paulie before she went to find Jenny?

4. If you were Anna, whom would you hold responsible for this situation, Paulie or Jenny? Explain.

5. Is this type of jealousy common? What are some ways to end jealousy in a relationship?

Violence
& Bias

The Evening News

Topic
violence and HIV

Character
Newsperson

NEWSPERSON *sits at an anchor desk and reads the story into a television camera.*

NEWSPERSON: A fifteen-year-old Boulder, Colorado, girl is being held at the city's Adolescent Psychiatric Center following an argument in which she allegedly shot and killed a fifteen-year-old classmate.

According to Boulder police, Evelyn Leonard, a tenth grader at Clairmont High School, shot Julia Mirandi at close range with a .22-caliber pistol. The incident took place in the school's cafeteria.

Witnesses say Mirandi was allegedly teasing Leonard about her father, who had recently been diagnosed HIV-positive. "Julia was always saying stuff about other people," a witness stated. "She started telling everybody that this girl's father had AIDS. Evelyn got real upset and ran out of the cafeteria. The next day Julia started in again but this time, Evelyn took a gun out of her backpack and shot her. Everybody ran. It was real scary."

Police corroborated the fact that Mirandi's alleged taunting led to the argument which resulted in her fatal shooting.

Because the suspect is only fifteen years old, she has been remanded to the Pine Valley School for Girls pending the results of a court-ordered psychiatric evaluation.

Discussion

1. Why could the shooting be termed a "bias crime"?

2. If Evelyn Leonard is found guilty of the shooting, how do you think she should she be punished?

3. Do you think the results of the psychiatric evaluation should have any impact on Evelyn's punishment?

4. Should the fact that Evelyn is only fifteen years old have an impact on her punishment?

5. Where do you think Evelyn got the gun she used in the shooting? Do you think Evelyn's parents should be held responsible in any way should it turn out that she used their gun? Explain.

Vanessa*

Topic
violence and sexual orientation

Characters
Vanessa, a junior in high school
Two friends who are seniors:
    Bobbie
    Jackie
Mr. Reynolds, a teacher on cafeteria duty
Cafeteria aide

> BOBBIE *and* JACKIE *sit at a cafeteria table, having lunch.* VANESSA *comes in alone and sits at the next table.*

BOBBIE: (*Surprised to see* VANESSA *in school*) Look, look—it's her.

JACKIE: Who? (*Begins to turn around*)

BOBBIE: No, don't turn around, she'll know we're talking about her.

JACKIE: I don't care who knows I'm talking about them. I talk about everybody! (*Turns and looks at* VANESSA) I can't believe it. Who does she think she is to show her face around here?

---

* This scene contains offensive language.

BOBBIE: Maybe she doesn't think that anyone knows.

JACKIE: Yeah, right. She put it in the literary magazine. The whole school knows.

BOBBIE: Well, maybe she doesn't think that anyone cares!

JACKIE: Believe me, people care about a thing like that. I mean if she wrote a dumb poem about feeling sad or wanting to kill herself or something, then nobody would care. But to write a poem about that. She knew she was going to raise a few eyebrows. She has some nerve.

BOBBIE: (*Parroting* JACKIE) Yeah, she has some nerve. I don't know about you, Jackie, but I feel weird being around her.

JACKIE: Me, too.

BOBBIE: I feel like she is gonna be looking at me all the time or something. (JACKIE *turns to look at* VANESSA.) Is she looking at us?

JACKIE: No, she's eating her lunch and reading a book.

BOBBIE: I still feel weird. I don't think it's right that they allow her in school with us normal people.

JACKIE: Especially after she comes out and announces it to the whole world. She is just asking for trouble.

BOBBIE: I guess the school district can't do anything about it.

JACKIE: (*With a look of disgust*) But we can.

BOBBIE: What do you mean?

JACKIE: Watch. (JACKIE *gets up from her table and moves to* VANESSA's *table. She sits directly across from* VANESSA *and furtively motions for* BOBBIE *to join her.* VANESSA *looks up briefly, recognizes trouble, and returns to her book.* JACKIE *addresses her, too sweetly.*) Hi, Vanessa.

BOBBIE: Hi, Vanessa.

VANESSA *ignores them.*

JACKIE: What're ya reading?

VANESSA *does not answer.*

BOBBIE: Yeah, what're ya reading, Vanessa?

Once again VANESSA *does not answer.*

JACKIE: (*Under her breath but with as much venom as she can muster*) Is it a story about another dyke?

VANESSA *knew something like this was coming, but the word "dyke" was like a punch in the stomach. She puts the book down, looks at the two girls, but then, with a great deal of effort, looks back to her book and resumes reading. Both* BOBBIE *and* JACKIE *are surprised at the response.* BOBBIE *picks up where* JACKIE *left off.*

BOBBIE: Or are you reading a *poem* about a *dyke*, like the one you wrote in the literary magazine?

JACKIE: Let's see. (*She grabs the book out of* VANESSA's *hands.*)

VANESSA: (*Struggling to maintain her composure*) Give me back the book!

BOBBIE: Not until you tell us what it's about.

VANESSA: That's none of your business. Now, give it back.

VANESSA *reaches for it and misses.* JACKIE *and* BOBBIE *laugh.*

JACKIE: All right. We'll give it back if you answer one question. (VANESSA *says nothing. She continues to stare at the two girls. She is quickly losing patience.*) So what do dykes read, anyway?

VANESSA: Stop using that word.

BOBBIE: Why? I think it's pretty descriptive.

VANESSA: Only ignorant jerks like you would call someone a *dyke* or a *nigger* or a *spic.*

JACKIE: I may be ignorant and I may be a jerk, but honey, I sure ain't no lesbian!

BOBBIE: (*Quietly cooing*) Queer.

JACKIE: Faggot.

Finally at the end of her patience, VANESSA *reaches across the table to take her book back.* JACKIE *refuses to let go and the two girls begin to struggle. The struggle turns into a full-fledged fight.* MR. REYNOLDS *and the* CAFETERIA AIDE *run over to separate the two girls.*

MR. REYNOLDS: All right, all right. Break it up. Girls, stop it! (*He succeeds in separating them*)

BOBBIE: It was Vanessa's fault, Mr. Reynolds. She just reached over the table and started hitting Jackie. I saw everything.

MR. REYNOLDS: Is that what happened, Vanessa?

VANESSA *says nothing, but she shakes her head "no." She continues to stare with anger at the two girls.*

JACKIE: What's the matter, the dyke lost her voice?

MR. REYNOLDS: (*Angry, speaking to* JACKIE) That's enough! I see there's more to this. Both of you, we're going down to the office. Come on. (*They leave.*)

CAFETERIA AIDE: (*To* BOBBIE) What was that all about?

BOBBIE: If they didn't let freaks into this school, things like this wouldn't happen.

CAFETERIA AIDE: What do you mean?

BOBBIE: Forget it. (*She walks away.*)

Discussion

1. Why do you think that Bobbie and Jackie want to cause Vanessa trouble?

2. Should Vanessa have published such a personal poem in the literary magazine? Was she asking for trouble, as Jackie says?

3. Explain how the language Jackie and Bobbie used was abusive.

4. What role does "tolerance" play in situations like this?

5. What are some things that a school might do to prevent situations like this from happening? What might students do?

The Prom*

Topic
violence and racism

Characters
Judy, a high school senior
Mrs. Duffy, the senior class advisor

> MRS. DUFFY *is in her room, finishing up some paperwork. The prom is in two weeks and arrangements need to be finalized.* JUDY *pops her head into the room to make sure that* MRS. DUFFY *is alone before she enters.*

JUDY: Mrs. Duffy?

MRS. DUFFY: *(Not looking up)* Just a minute...Fifty one, fifty two, fifty three...There. *(Looking up and seeing* JUDY, *she is a bit befuddled.)* Oh, Judy. I'm sorry, but this is important. Very important! I was in the middle of counting prom favors. Look, it's a little stuffed falcon. At least it's supposed to be a falcon. People would be pretty upset if they thought our school mascot was a buzzard. What do you think?

JUDY: I think it looks fine. Uh, I wanted to—

---

* This scene contains offensive language.

106

MRS. DUFFY: (*Not meaning to interrupt her, but a bit overwhelmed with all the details*) We are going to have to put a stuffed falcon at each place setting and make sure that people take only one each. We only ordered enough for one per person, of course...

JUDY: (*Still holding the stuffed animal*) Uh, Mrs. Duffy...

MRS. DUFFY: Maybe we will have to tie each one to the...

JUDY: (*Putting two prom tickets on* MRS. DUFFY's *desk*) Mrs. Duffy, I'm not going to the prom.

MRS. DUFFY: (JUDY *has gotten her attention.*) What?

JUDY: That's what I came in to tell you. I need to return the tickets. I know it's late and if you can't give me my money back I understand.

MRS. DUFFY: (*Reluctantly taking the tickets*) What do you mean you're not going? You have worked so hard with the class council to make this the best prom in years! You can't miss it!

JUDY: Well, something came up.

MRS. DUFFY: What came up? I know it's none of my business, but I am concerned about this.

JUDY: Just something, Ok. I really can't talk about it now. Look, I gotta go. Keep the tickets. Let me know if you can get a refund.

JUDY *turns and begins to walk to the door.* MRS. DUFFY *is upset, and she tries to decide whether she should say anything further. Just as* JUDY *is about to leave the room,* MRS. DUFFY *stops her.*

MRS. DUFFY: Judy. Is all this about Charlie?

JUDY *stops and turns to* MRS. DUFFY.

JUDY: What do you mean?

MRS. DUFFY: Honey, come on back in and close the door. I have been hearing a few people talking about it but I just dismissed it as the ignorant talk of ignorant people. I was hoping that the two of you were doing the same.

JUDY: Listen Mrs. Duffy, over the past two years both Charlie and I have become pretty numb about this. Kids at school, people at the movies, even some of our own families have said things to us that I would never repeat here. We let most of if just roll off our backs.

MRS. DUFFY: Then what's the problem? I know that you and Charlie have a lot of good friends who are going with you to the prom. You don't have to bother with anything anyone else is saying. Does Charlie know you're here?

JUDY: No. He doesn't know anything about this.

MRS. DUFFY: (*Thinking she has solved the problem, she hands* JUDY *back her tickets.*) Then why don't you take these back and we'll just attribute this to a bout of momentary cold feet.

JUDY: It's not that easy, Mrs. Duffy. (*Instead of taking the tickets, she hands* MRS. DUFFY *a folded note*) I found this in my locker yesterday afternoon.

MRS. DUFFY: (*Taking the note and reading it aloud*) "We don't want no niggers mixing with white people in this town." (*She pauses, very upset*) Did you show this to anyone?

JUDY: No.

MRS. DUFFY: Does Charlie know about it?

JUDY: No. He'd just get crazy.

MRS. DUFFY: So why did you show it to me?

JUDY: I don't know. I first thought that I should just ignore it. Probably nothing will happen at the prom, and if something does, Charlie is certainly big enough to handle it. Then I thought that the people who wrote this would probably be the ones who show up at every dance drunk out of their minds. Who could predict what would happen with a bunch of drunks? So I decided that the best thing to do would be just not to go. I'd tell Charlie I was sick or something. He would be real disappointed, but we would be avoiding any chance of a problem.

MRS. DUFFY: Are you comfortable with that decision?

JUDY: What do you mean?

MRS. DUFFY: Are you comfortable with not going to a prom that you worked so hard to plan because you want to avoid a problem?

JUDY: You mean you want us to go and risk getting into a horrible fight or something? I don't think it's worth it. Do you?

MRS. DUFFY: Absolutely not. But are those your only options? Think about it for a minute.

JUDY: I've thought about it enough. I want nothing to do with this school, this prom, or these people. If they can't accept our relationship, that's their problem.

MRS. DUFFY: Judy, that's fine for now. It's fine for next week. But what if your relationship with Charlie lasts for several years? You are going to come up against a lot of ugly people who are going to threaten to do a lot of ugly things.

JUDY: Now you've got me really confused.

MRS. DUFFY: I know. Things like this are not easy to get a handle on. Just listen for a minute. You obviously can't go to the prom and wind up in a fight. That's not an option. But, on the other hand, you can't run away. Running away from these people would be like conceding to their ignorance and hate! And you can't keep running away from racism or violence all your life. You have to confront it!

JUDY: Confronting it means a fight!

MRS. DUFFY: You bet. We've got to fight this with everything we've got. You said yourself you have tough skin and I've never known you to walk away from a problem.

JUDY: I know, but—

MRS. DUFFY: But that doesn't mean we need to crack any heads open.

JUDY: Then what kind of fight are you talking about?

MRS. DUFFY: I'm talking about the kind you do with your brains instead of your fists.

JUDY: What are you thinking of?

MRS. DUFFY: I don't know yet, exactly. Give me a minute and I know that I will come up with something that will turn this ugly thing around.

JUDY: I hope you're right

MRS. DUFFY: So do I. We have to be positive!

JUDY: So what do I do now?

MRS. DUFFY: (*Handing her back the tickets*) The first thing you do is take back these tickets. Now, go get Charlie. We all have some serious talking to do.

JUDY: (*Begins to leave*) He's getting extra help in chemistry... (*Notices that she has been clutching the stuffed prom favor for the entire time. She moves to give it back to* MRS. DUFFY) Oh, here, I almost took him with me. I don't want to mess up your count.

MRS. DUFFY: Keep it. I have more important things to think about now than how many stuffed buzzards we have!

JUDY: Falcons, Mrs. Duffy. Think positive. (*She leaves.*)

MRS. DUFFY: (*To herself*) I'm trying to, honey. I'm trying to.

Discussion

1. Is Mrs. Duffy doing the right thing when she suggests to Judy that a confrontation is needed? What type of confrontation is Mrs. Duffy talking about? Isn't she just asking for more trouble?

2. What would you have done had you found a similar note in your locker? Would you still go to the prom? Explain.

3. Name something that Mrs. Duffy might suggest to Judy to ease the situation. Who else would you involve to help you with the problem?

4. Do you know of any similar problems that have resulted from interracial dating? Explain.

Andy*

Topic
violence and sexual orientation

Characters
Andy, a freshman in high school
Boy 1
Boy 2
Girl 1

> ANDY *stands center stage.* BOY 1, BOY 2, *and* GIRL 1 *stand around* ANDY *in a triangle formation. They are all facing the audience, looking straight ahead, and they all speak directly to the audience.*

BOY 1: Faggot.

GIRL 1: Wimp.

BOY 2: Queer.

ANDY: (*Pause*) It's like that every day. They never stop. I don't understand. I never did anything to them. I don't even know most of them.

GIRL 1: (*Sarcastically*) Hey, Andy, how about bein' with me this weekend—just you and me? What do you say, honey? Are ya up for it? (*Laughs*)

---

* This scene contains offensive language.

ANDY: I'm gay. I know it and they know it. But it's nobody's business but mine.

BOY 1: Queer!

ANDY: But for some reason they think they have to make fun of me, to call me names, to hurt me some way. Why? Do I threaten them?

BOY 2: He's just not normal.

BOY 1: He's not like us.

GIRL 1: He's a homo!

ANDY: So what? Why do they all care so much? I don't bother them. It's not like I'm trying to pick anybody up in gym or anything. I avoid people like them because I know they can cause trouble. I know how fast their stupid name-calling can turn into—

BOY 2: Hey, Andy, you better not sit next to me in Health again or I'll beat your ass.

BOY 1: Or me either, queer boy. You remember what happened last time.

ANDY: (*To himself*) I remember.

GIRL 1: (*Again, sarcastically*) You can sit by me, Andy. Better yet, why don't you let me sit on your lap? You'd like that, wouldn't you? Oh, no, come to think of it, you wouldn't.

They all laugh.

ANDY: Even some of the girls can be really cruel. Listen, not everybody is out to get me. I have some really great friends—male and female—both gay and straight. And even some of the teachers are cool. They know what's going on and they are usually supportive. But you know, I even get bad feelings from a few of the teachers—like they're judging me or something. What right does anybody have to judge anybody else?

BOY 2 AND GIRL 1: But he's not normal!

ANDY: It's tough sometimes. To ignore them, I mean. Sometimes you just gotta say something back to them and then—

BOY 1: Hey, faggot, where's your dress? (*All laugh*)

ANDY: (*To the three students*) Shut the hell up!

They are all surprised that they have gotten a rise out of ANDY. *They turn and look at one another. He has finally given them the opportunity they have all been waiting for.*

BOY 1: What?

GIRL 1: What did he say?

BOY 2: Was he talking to us?

ANDY: I said leave me and my friends alone. We're not bothering you.

BOY 2: (*Sarcastically and menacingly*) My, my, my. The little gay boy *was* talking to us.

GIRL 1: Well, boys, are you going to take that from the little wimp?

BOY 1: Hell no!

GIRL 1: What should we do?

The three students pause and look at one another in "mock thought." Then, with all the glee of a lynch mob, they shout...

ALL: Get him!

There is a fast blackout.

Discussion

1. Why do you think that gay students are frequent targets of intolerance and violence in schools?

2. Do you think that gay students should be open about their homosexuality? Explain.

3. What could students like Andy do to avoid further problems in school?

4. What could students who are not gay do to help students like Andy avoid problems in school?

Harper Lee Revisited*

Topic
violence and racism

Character
Tonya, a high school sophomore

> TONYA *sits on a stool and speaks directly to the audience.*

TONYA: It happened a couple of months ago, but it seems like it just happened yesterday.

We were reading this great book in class called *To Kill a Mockingbird* by Harper Lee. It's all about the South during the depression and this black guy who is on trial for raping a white woman—he didn't do it. Anyway, Harper Lee really makes you feel like you are in Alabama in the 30s; or that you're really looking at a rabid dog walking down the street; or that you're terrified of this guy named Boo Radley who hasn't come out of his house in fifteen years.

Harper Lee writes the way people talked back then, and that includes a lot of people using the word "nigger." I am not going to lie to you. When I first heard Mr. Heck read

---

* This scene contains offensive language.

the word "nigger" aloud in class I kinda took a deep breath and looked out of the window. Mr. Heck is our English teacher and he really gets into it when he reads. He does a southern accent and everything. When he gets to a part where someone uses the word "nigger," he really spits it out. *"Nigger,"* he would hiss.

Now, being the only African-American in the class, everyone else would always look over to me to see if I was going to get up and pop him in the mouth or something. At first, I wanted to. Why did he have to say that word so loud? Why couldn't he just bounce over it real fast and get on with the rest of the story? Why did he have to make it ring in our ears? Then, after a week or so, I realized what he was doing. He was making the word "nigger" sound as evil as he possibly could. Maybe he thought that if he sneered every time he said it, the class would also realize how hateful it was.

Anyway, that sorta brings me to Phyllis and Amanda. Phyllis and Amanda are these two girls in my English class who hate my guts. I really don't know why they hate me so much. I think that it has something to do with the fact that I made the varsity cheerleading squad this year and they didn't. When they saw that they didn't make it, they were really mad and started saying that the tryouts were rigged and that the coach only picked her favorites. I never thought of myself as anyone's favorite. I thought that the tryouts were fair and that the girls who made the team were the ones who deserved to make it. Then, I made the mistake of saying that to Phyllis and Amanda.

The first time it happened was the day we were all reading about Helen Robinson—she's the wife of Tom Robinson. While Tom was in jail, Helen would have to walk to work past Bob Ewell's house. It was Ewell's daughter who accused Tom of raping her but nobody really believed her story. When Helen walked past the Ewell's house each morning, Bob would follow her and, as Harper Lee says, "say dirt to her." I could only imagine what "dirt" Bob Ewell was saying, but you could be damn sure that every couple of words must have been "nigger." That chapter left me with a bad feeling inside.

When the bell rang, I packed up and headed for gym. The halls were crowded and noisy but I thought I heard someone calling my name. "Tonya. Oh, Tonya." I turned and saw Phyllis and Amanda a couple of feet behind me, but they pretended not to see me. I kept walking.

"They shouldn't let niggers be varsity cheerleaders."

They hissed it, real quiet.

"Nigger."

I didn't know what to do so I kept walking. I felt like I had been punched in the stomach, so I just ignored them. They turned at the next corner and I went to gym. During gym, I decided to forget what happened and to stay away from them. I promised myself that I wasn't going to let ignorant people get the best of me.

The next day after English, it happened again. I was walking down the hall and I heard that hateful hissing. It was only Phyllis this time.

"I guess they had to put at least one nigger on the squad, even if she wasn't really good enough."

Without thinking I stopped, turned, and slapped her across the face as hard as I could. She hit me back and we were soon rolling around on the floor. A teacher and some other kids had to pull us apart. We both got five days out-of-school suspension for fighting. The principal said that he didn't care who said what to whom. Fighting was forbidden, period.

I know that it wasn't my fault. But I also know that I should have had more self-control. I just should have kept ignoring her. I should have been more like Helen Robinson. She kept walking, proud, like a lady, past that filthy Ewell.

But that's a lot of "shoulds" and real life isn't made up of "shoulds." All I can say is that the next time something like that happens, I'll try. I'll try to keep walking, with my head up...like Helen Robinson. But this time, I'm not making any promises.

Discussion

1. Why do you think that Phyllis and Amanda hate Tonya?

2. What motivates Phyllis and Amanda to harass Tonya? What reason would Phyllis and Amanda give? Explain.

3. What makes the word "nigger" so explosive?

4. Would you consider Tonya a victim or a survivor? Explain.

5. Is Tonya's solution of ignoring the problem copping out? Explain. Should she ever confront Phyllis and Amanda?

6. What would you have done had you been in Tonya's situation?

Violence
in Society

The Evening News #1

Topic
senseless violence

Character
Newsperson

NEWSPERSON *sits at an anchor desk and reads the story into a television camera.*

NEWSPERSON: In Bridgeport, Connecticut, yesterday, two teenagers were arrested for killing and mutilating a swan at a local park. Fifteen-year-old Anthony Donovan and sixteen-year-old Kris Susca have been charged with stabbing the swan over forty times, severing its head, and leaving the mutilated body on a park bench.

This act of brutality has upset the community because the mute swan, a park favorite, was protecting its nesting mate when attacked.

"Why would kids do something senseless like this?" asked a local resident. "Why are kids so violent today?"

The teenagers have offered no explanation for the killing but the police have said that alcohol was involved.

The father of one of the boys expressed his surprise over the attention this story has received in the press. Mr. Jody Donovan said, "People are being killed in this country every day! This was a duck! What's the big deal?"

Discussion

1. Do you think that kids are more violent today than they have been in the past? Explain.

2. Why do you think that the community is so upset over the death of the swan? After all, according to the father of one of the boys, "This was a duck!"

3. What details of the story make this particularly gruesome?

4. Why do you think the boys do this? How should they be punished?

Planning Funerals

Topic
violence and gangs

Characters
Alicia, 14
Christopher, 15
Elynore, 15
Jaime, 14
Miss Holt, a middle school social worker

Four middle school students are sitting in a circle in MISS HOLT's *office. This is the third time they have met as a discussion group that examines violence in their school and community. They all know one another well and feel comfortable enough to be honest.*

MISS HOLT: How's everyone doing today? Jaime, before we begin, I wanted to tell you that Mr. Warrens spoke with me yesterday.

JAIME: (*Annoyed*) What did he want? Why doesn't he mind his own business before somebody starts minding it for him? I mean, what does that guy want? I spent three hours studying for that stupid test and if that wasn't enough to make him happy, he can just—

MISS HOLT: Slow down, slow down. You are jumping to conclusions again. You don't even know what we spoke about. Why do you automatically assume the worst?

ELYNORE: (*Jumping in*) You live in this city long enough, you learn real early to always expect the worst!

They all laugh.

MISS HOLT: I know, but that is one of the things we were going to work on in here, remember? Anyway, before you flew into your rage, Jaime, I was going to tell you that you got a ninety-three on yesterday's unit test.

JAIME: A ninety-three?

ELYNORE: Go, girl!

CHRISTOPHER: You know what my father would say if I told him I got a ninety-three on that test? He'd say, "Why did you get seven wrong?"

ALICIA: (*Sarcastically*) Now, that's encouragement!

MISS HOLT: Jaime, a ninety-three is great. You *should* feel encouraged. That's why I think Mr. Warrens spoke to me. He wanted to let me know that he has been leaning on you pretty hard lately but that it paid off. He's real proud of you.

JAIME: He said that?

MISS HOLT: He said that.

JAIME: Damn!

MISS HOLT: Ok, now let's get to our other business. Last time we met, I asked you to write a journal entry about the effect the gangs in the city have had on you. Did everyone get a chance to do it? (*Some of them nod*) Ok. I also asked you to title your entry. Do me a favor, go around the circle and read off the titles. Jaime, you first.

JAIME: "Gangs and the Biology Unit Exam."

MISS HOLT: Seriously?

JAIME: Yup.

MISS HOLT: Ok. Chris.

CHRISTOPHER: "Gangs, Guns, and Goodfellas."

MISS HOLT: Alicia.

ALICIA: "I Want to Reach the Age of 21."

MISS HOLT: Good. And Elynore.

ELYNORE: "Planning the Funeral."

MISS HOLT: Planning whose funeral?

ELYNORE: Mine.

MISS HOLT: What do you mean?

ELYNORE: Well, my family and I have seen so many people we know get shot and killed that we must have planned a hundred funerals. So, I thought that I'd save everybody some time and energy and plan my own.

MISS HOLT: Do you want to read it for us?

ELYNORE: Sure. "They all say I'm too young. They say that I have my whole life in front of me. They say it'll never happen to me. I used to think that too. Then I saw my brother get shot while he was standing on the corner waiting for his girlfriend. They say that some gang members drove by, thought he was someone they were after and shot him. He died right there on the curb. Now, at night, when I'm trying to go to sleep, I think about my brother. I think about his funeral. And I have started to think about my own funeral. I only weigh about eighty-five pounds so I won't need a big casket. I want one that is black and red. I want to hold the Bible that my Grandma gave me. I don't want them to close the cover. I want it open so that I can see who comes to the wake. And I want the people who killed me to be able to see me, too. I want them to hear my Mamma and my sisters crying. After my brother got killed, I felt funny. I felt sad and everything, but I also felt that it wasn't fair. I felt that these people with their guns stole my brother from me and my family. They took him from us, just like they'd steal a pack of cigarettes from the store— without even thinking. That's why I'm planning my funeral. I want to be ready when it's my turn." (*To* MISS HOLT) Does that make any sense?

MISS HOLT: It makes a whole lot of sense, honey. Thank you.

Discussion

1. Why do you think that Jamie expected to fail the biology test? Do you think that this expectation is at all related to Elynore's journal entry? Explain.

2. Do you ever think about your death? Are these thoughts "normal?" Are they similar to what Elynore wrote about? Explain.

3. Why would it be all right to think about death but not all right to go so far as to plan your own funeral?

4. Describe the feelings a fourteen year old must have to make her/him think s/he may die at a young age.

A Friend in Need

Topic
violence as entertainment

Characters
Two sixteen-year-old boys:
    Alex
    Sean

> *The stage is dark. The audience hears two disembodied voices.*

SEAN: (*With excitement*) Wait, wait, I'll help you. Keep him pinned down until I get there.

ALEX: (*With equal excitement but also with a sense of urgency*) Hurry up, he's gonna get away. He's stronger than me...Come on...He's gonna kill me...

SEAN: I'm coming...I'm...there...(*Accompanied by the grunt of an unseen kick*) There!

ALEX: Kick him again, he's getting up...

SEAN: (*With enthusiasm punctuating each kick*) Ah!... Ah!...Ah! There! He ain't going nowhere.

ALEX: Come on, let's get outta here. I have the feeling that some of his friends might be hanging around and I don't want them to find us here.

SEAN: Watch out!

ALEX: Where?

SEAN: Behind the light pole—

ALEX: (*Screaming in pain*) Ahhh! He's on my back...

SEAN: He's got a knife...Watch out...

ALEX: Get him off me...He's gonna...

SEAN: No he's not. Not if I can get my knife into him first... (*As he stabs into the opponent's back*) Yes... Yes...Yes.

ALEX: (*Screaming in pain*) Ahhh, he stabbed me...

SEAN: (*Again, with urgency*) Where?

ALEX: I don't know, but...Ahhh...He stabbed me again... Get him...He's gonna kill me!

SEAN: Ok, I'm coming over.

ALEX: Quick...I'm dying here.

SEAN: Damn it!

ALEX: Sean, help me...I'm bleeding to death... Sean, please...

SEAN: I can't.

ALEX: (*With desperation*) What do you mean you can't, I'm almost dead!

SEAN: I don't have any more quarters.

ALEX: (*Annoyed, breaking the urgent tone in his voice*) Every time you're dying I always manage to get you out of it, but every time they get me pinned down, you run out of quarters. Some best friend you are.

SEAN: Sorry, Alex, but I've been on this machine for almost half an hour and I ran out of money.

ALEX: But I really wanted to rip that guy's head off today!

SEAN: Maybe tomorrow.

ALEX: Yeah, maybe. See you tomorrow, Sean.

SEAN: See ya. And Alex...

ALEX: Yea?

SEAN: I won't let 'em kill you tomorrow, I promise.

ALEX: (*Unenthusiastically*) Thanks.

SEAN: Don't mention it.

Discussion

1. Do you think that it's a problem that the two boys got so involved in the video game?

2. Do you think that the violent realism of some video games is a problem?

3. Why do you think certain video games have become so violent?

4. Even though playing video games has taken on a negative connotation, are there any positive aspects to playing video games? Explain.

5. Do you think that the violence in video games spills over into society? Explain.

Child's Play

Topic
violence as entertainment

Characters
Two teenagers:
    Ellen
    Greg
Martin, their seven- year-old brother

> ELLEN *and* GREG *have taken* MARTIN *to a video store to rent a video game. They are all standing in front of the selections, trying to decide which game to bring home.*

MARTIN: (*Excitedly*) Look, here's that new one called "Rip Out His Guts." I want that one, Ellen.

ELLEN: I don't know, Martin, that one sounds just a little bit too bloody for a seven year old.

MARTIN: What do you mean too bloody?

GREG: You remember what Mom told us, Martin. She doesn't want you to play any of the really violent games.

MARTIN: She still thinks I'm a baby. Look at the cover of the box, this guy's getting his guts ripped out! Cool!

ELLEN: Uh, Martin, I don't think so.

MARTIN: (*Reluctantly putting the box down*) Oh, all right. How about this one?. (*Picks up another box*). "Vigilante Kick Boxers." This one looks cool, too.

ELLEN: Let's see. I've never heard of this one. Do you know anything about it, Greg?

GREG: Yeah, I played it over Tom's house. It's not that bad. The only bad thing is if the bad guy kicks you in the head more than four times your head falls off and blood spurts all over the place, that's all.

MARTIN: Cool!

ELLEN: No way! Pick another one, Martin.

MARTIN: (*Pleading*) Oh, Ellen.

ELLEN: No. Mom would kill me if you brought that home. Pick another one.

GREG: Here's one. "Warrior Chickens From The Next Galaxy."

ELLEN: Let me see. (*Looking at the back of the box to preview sample game screens*) This one doesn't look too bad. These chickens are invading Earth and you have to fight to save the planet.

MARTIN: Cool, chickens from space!

ELLEN: (*Reading*) "You and your friends must save Earth by turning these pesky pieces of poultry into chicken nuggets!"

MARTIN: Neat!

ELLEN: Wait a minute. In order to win the game you have to catch the chickens, cut their heads off, and deep-fry them. Greg, look at these graphics!

GREG: (*Looking*) Looks like fun.

MARTIN: Let me see. Let me see!

ELLEN: Absolutely not!

MARTIN: Ellen, you never let me have any fun.

GREG: Yeah, Ellen, lighten up. It's only a game.

ELLEN: (*Trying to change the topic*) Hey, look, here's a good one. "Itty Bitty Bear And Her Forest Friends."

MARTIN: (*Looking at the box with disgust*) Ah, that's for kids.

ELLEN: What exactly do you think you are?

MARTIN: I'm a kid, but that's for *little* kids.

ELLEN: I see.

GREG: (*Finding another game*) Wait a minute, I think I found a good one.

MARTIN: What's the name of it?

GREG: "Video Maniac."

ELLEN: Look on the back of the box. Is it really violent?

GREG: I'm looking. No, I don't think so.

ELLEN: Any decapitations?

GREG: Nope.

ELLEN: Any spurting jugulars?

GREG: Nope.

ELLEN: Any butchering of small, flying animals?

GREG: Nope. It looks like the only violent thing is that you get to chop the bad guy's legs off if you win.

MARTIN: Cool!

ELLEN: Only his legs?

GREG: Oh, and his arms, too.

ELLEN: That's it?

GREG: Yup.

MARTIN: Let's get it, let's get it!

ELLEN: Ok, ok. It doesn't sound too bad.

MARTIN: Thanks, Ellen. (*Grabs the box and runs to the cashier*)

ELLEN *and* GREG *begin to slowly follow* MARTIN.

ELLEN: Were toys this violent when we were kids?

GREG: We had GI Joe and guns and stuff.

ELLEN: Yeah, but they were nothing like some of these video games they're coming out with now. I wonder if all of this violence has any effect on kids Martin's age?

GREG: Nah, they know it's only a game. Kids can tell the difference between reality and video.

ELLEN: I hope you're right.

MARTIN *comes running up, excited with the prospect of playing the new game.*

MARTIN: Come on you guys, I want to get home.

ELLEN: We're coming.

MARTIN: Hey, Greg?

GREG: Yeah, Martin?

MARTIN: Are you gonna play this with me when we get home?

GREG: Sure.

MARTIN: Great! How long do you think it will take me to chop off your arms and your legs, huh? How long? Do you think I have to chop off one leg at a time or can I get 'em both in one big swoop? I wish I could chop off your head, too. I want to see your blood spurting all over.

ELLEN *looks at* GREG. GREG *is concerned. They all walk out of the store slowly.*

Discussion

1. Do you think that there is a connection between playing violent video games and violent behavior? Explain.

2. Should Martin be able to play any game he chooses, regardless of the level of violence? Explain.

3. Should explicitly violent games be banned? What about the censorship issue when it comes to violence and video games?

The Wolf Pack

Topic
gangs

Characters
Four teenage boys ranging in age from thirteen to seventeen
Reporter from a city newspaper

> *The four boys are positioned around the stage, facing forward and speaking directly to the audience. The reporter stands in the middle of the stage and reads from a newspaper article.*

1: They're my friends.

2: They're cool.

3: We hang out.

4: They're my family.

REPORTER: In the past six months, the city has seen an increase in what has been called by police as "wolf pack crime."

1: We watch out for each other.

2: We work together.

3: We're a unit.

4: We do what needs to be done.

REPORTER: Wolf pack crime involves groups of teenagers, usually ranging in age from twelve to fifteen, who rob individuals. Much like wolves in a pack, they pick solitary victims, isolate them, surround them, then rob them.

1: Clothes, man. We all need clothes.

2: You think this stuff's cheap?

3: My mother don't have no money to give me. What do you expect me to do, get a job?

4: Jobs suck, man. You do all this work for nothing. They pay you nothing. It's just not worth it.

REPORTER: Most wolf pack crime take place in isolated areas of the city such as train platforms or empty streets. Ironically, many of the victims are teenagers themselves.

1: I didn't hit him, I swear!

2: Everybody else got him. I just stood there.

3: I said, "Just give us your money" and he started yelling.

4: Somebody had to shut him up.

REPORTER: In 1987, kids under sixteen committed 1,900 robberies in New York City. In 1992, the number rose to 3,900. The numbers are expected only to increase.

1: So, we bashed him a little.

2: Big deal.

3: What's a little blood? He didn't die or nothin'.

4: Too bad he only had five bucks on him.

REPORTER: Police and city officials are at a loss to explain why teenagers are turning to violent crime. Many experts cite poverty and hopelessness as reasons. A sense of "fatalism" also plays a role in the desperation found in so many of today's young people.

1: My brother was in a gang when he was fourteen. He was shot in the head. I was only seven, only a kid, but you remember something like that. I'm seventeen now. I've lasted for five years. Who knows how long I can hold out?

2: My mother threw me out of the house when I was fifteen. I've been living on the streets for almost a year. I have seen people get shot and I have seen 'em die—right in front of me. You gotta get tough or you won't make it.

3: My cousin got me into it. My mother doesn't know. All she keeps saying is, "Where you been all night? You didn't come home. You're only thirteen years old! You gotta go to school in the morning." She don't understand.

4: I've been arrested seven times. They all know me by now. All the cops kid me that I'm gonna break my brother's record. He's been arrested ten times already. I don't care. Why should I care?

REPORTER: A common theme that emerges time after time with these kids is a sense of their own mortality. They have seen death so many times that their own untimely death becomes a given. When you are not afraid to die, you are afraid of little else.

4: I wanted to be a doctor, like my cousin Bobby, but, shit, that'll never happen now.

3: I won this city writing contest when I was in third grade. The topic was "Reaching for the Stars." What a joke.

2: We were gonna move out of the city when I was a kid. We had a house picked out and everything. But then my dad left and that was the end of that.

1: I just want to see my brother again.

REPORTER: Whatever the reasons, these children have learned to survive in their violent world. Indeed, like wolves, they have turned to each other for support, for protection, and for love. Can the city honestly offer them anything better?

1: They're my friends.

2: They're cool.

3: We hang out.

ALL: We're a family.

Discussion

1. Define "fatalism." How does the idea of fatalism play a significant role in the lives of these teenagers? What causes this fatalism? What can be done to change a fatalistic attitude?

2. Why do you think that the numbers of violent crimes committed by teenagers has greatly increased over the past several years?

3. How do these teenagers rationalize their violence?

4. What does "these kids have a sense of their own mortality" mean?

The Evening News #2

Topic
guns and teenagers

Character
Newsperson

> NEWSPERSON *sits at an anchor desk and reads the story into a television camera.*

NEWSPERSON: A fourteen-year-old girl was shot and killed inside a dance club last night when an argument broke out between two unidentified men. Five other people, including three teenagers under eighteen, were also wounded.

The incident took place sometime after midnight at "The Pit," on the corner of Third Avenue and Grand Street. Officers at the scene discovered shells from a nine millimeter semiautomatic pistol scattered over the dance floor.

According to eyewitnesses, two men in their late twenties began arguing in the middle of the dance floor. The argument quickly escalated and one of the men pulled out a gun and began spraying the dance floor with gunfire.

Maria Lopez, fourteen, was caught in the crossfire and died of her injuries at Good Samaritan Hospital.

Pamela Lopez, Maria's cousin, was next to Maria when the shooting began. She said her cousin loved to dance. "That's why she was here. She wasn't looking for trouble. She was just a kid. She loved to come here, listen to the music, and dance. She would dance for hours. There was never trouble like this here before. Never."

Another witness to the shooting was Peter Milano, the club's manager. "These guys were lunatics. Real crazy," he said in an interview at the club. "Some people call guys like this 'mad agents.' They are people who will shoot you because you looked at them wrong or because you accidentally bumped into them or something. We usually get good people in here, but you can never tell who is carrying a gun these days." When asked why so many under-age teenagers were in the club, Mr. Milan said that everyone who enters the club is checked for a valid ID. "If she was in here, she had an ID. That's all I know."

Others at the club said that the management let in many under-age teenagers and regularly sold them alcohol.

At her apartment, Maria's mother, Lydia, sat surrounded by her family. "She was a good girl. She was so young. She was my baby. How could something like this happen? They should not have allowed her in that place. She was only fourteen years old. How could this happen?"

Two fifteen-year-old boys as well as a
sixteen-year- old girl were also wounded.
As of today, police say they have no suspects.

Discussion

1. What is a "mad agent?" Do you know of anyone who could be
   called a "mad agent?" Explain.

2. Why is it important that the man who allegedly fired the gun
   was described as a "mad agent?"

3. Is it significant that Maria Lopez was only fourteen years old?
   Does the fact that the club regularly admits under-age teenagers have anything to do with the violence that occurred?

More at 11:00

Topic
violence, death, and mourning

Characters
Jerry Miller, a TV reporter
Robert Phelan, principal of Albany Middle School
Classmates of Bobby Baptista:
  Jose
  Eva

> JERRY MILLER *is standing outside the Grayson Methodist Church. He is interviewing* PRINCIPAL PHELAN *about the memorial service that is about to take place for one of his ninth-grade students.*

MILLER: (*Looking into a camera and speaking into a mike*) We are here, live, at the steps of the Grayson Methodist Church speaking with Robert Phelan, principal of Albany Middle School. In back of us, you can see several hundred junior high school students entering the church. These students have been bused here for the memorial service of one of their classmates. (*Turning to the principal*) Mr. Phelan, could you give us some details surrounding the memorial service?

PHELAN: (*Holding a gallon jug of coins*) Yes, we are here today to remember Bobby Baptista, a

student from our school who was killed a
few days ago.

MILLER: How many students have you bused here
today?

PHELAN: As many as wanted to come. I didn't count.
But I would think that there are several
hundred.

MILLER: Why did you allow them to come?

PHELAN: Well, the atmosphere at school is somber, as
you might guess. Bobby was a popular
boy—very well liked. Many students are
taking his death very hard. We thought that
allowing them to attend the memorial
service might help them deal with Bobby's
death. We thought that it might be some
sort of catharsis for them.

MILLER: And how did the boy die?

PHELAN: I don't have all the details. You will have to
ask the police about it.

MILLER: Isn't it true that he was shot and killed
during an attempted holdup at an ATM?

PHELAN: I think so, yes.

MILLER: Isn't it also true that he was holding a pellet
gun, which the police mistook for a pistol?

PHELAN: Yes, I believe so.

MILLER: How old was Bobby when he died?

PHELAN: Fifteen.

MILLER: I see that you are holding a water jug full of
coins. Could you tell us what it is for?

PHELAN: Well, it seems that the Baptista family is
currently experiencing financial problems.
So some students began collecting money
to help. I am holding one jug and other staff

members have three more. I think the
students raised close to three hundred
dollars.

MILLER: I hear that your school is also doing other
things to help the students cope with this
tragedy.

PHELAN: Yes. The flag has been flying at half-mast all
week, several school social workers have
been meeting with students who would like
to talk, and we have begun to talk about
ways to create a memorial for Bobby at the
school.

MILLER: Mr. Phelan, do you have any problem with
the fact that you are doing all of this for a
boy who was killed in the process of
committing a crime? He was, after all,
waving what looked like a loaded gun!

PHELAN: A death is a death, Mr. Miller, no matter
what the circumstances. Whether he died in
a car crash or of a fatal disease, a death is a
death. And when a fifteen year old dies, it's
a tragedy. When he dies of a gunshot
wound, it's an even greater tragedy.

MILLER: Thank you, Mr. Phelan. (*Turning to two
students who are standing on his left*) We also
have with us two students who were Bobby's
classmates, Eva Lopez and Jose Minuto. Eva,
what can you tell us about Bobby?

EVA: I knew him since we were in third grade.
He was a nice guy. He used to hang out
with me and my brother. I think it was a
dare—the robbery, I mean. He wouldn't
have done something like this on his own. I
think some older kids put him up to it.

MILLER: And, Jose?

JOSE: What he did was wrong. You can't go around holding people up with pellet guns. But did he have to die for it?

MILLER: Thank you. I see that the service is about to begin. Police have told me that they are continuing to investigate the shooting, and the officer responsible has been placed on modified assignment until the investigation is complete. Tonight, we will have the story of some parents who are outraged about the fact that the school has used buses to bring their children to this memorial service. They consider Bobby Baptista a criminal and that the school district is sending the wrong message to their children by honoring his death. More at 11. Now, back to the studio.

Discussion

1. Do you think that the actions of the school district could be considered "honoring Bobby's death?"

2. Should the school district have responded at all to Bobby's death? What is the reason they give for the actions they take?

3. Define "catharsis." How would attending the memorial service be a type of "catharsis" for Bobby's classmates?

4. Do you agree with Principal Phelan when he says, "a death is a death?" Explain.

5. Should it make any difference to the school or to the parents that Bobby was killed in the process of robbing someone at an ATM?

The Graduation Party

Topic
violence, alcohol, and guns

Characters
Jaime Masters, an eighteen year old who has just graduated from
   high school
Mr. Masters
Mrs. Masters
Alan, Jaime's younger brother
Michele, Jaime's girlfriend
Walker, a twenty-year-old uninvited guest
Walker's friends
a house full of teenagers

> *It's one a.m. and* JAIME's *graduation party has
> been in full swing for several hours. In fact, more
> people are showing up who have not been invited
> and more people are arriving drunk.* JAIME's *par-
> ents are in the process of trying to bring the party
> to a close.*

MRS. MASTERS: *(Hurrying downstairs to the party in the
basement, upset and calling for her son)* Jaime!
Jaime! This is getting out of hand. Did you
invite all these people?

JAIME: No, Ma, they just sorta crashed.

MRS. MASTERS: And there are more people outside on the
front lawn. Your father is out there right
now trying to get them to leave. I want you

to tell these people down here that the party's over. Tell them it's time to go home! It's one in the morning!

JAIME: Ok, Mom, calm down! I'll start to wind things down. I'll get them out of here. Relax!

MRS. MASTERS: Good, good. I'll go up to help your father.

MRS. MASTERS goes back upstairs. JAIME finds his girlfriend and his brother to help him with the crowd.

JAIME: Hey, guys. Things are starting to get a little crazy and my parents are starting to flip. Help me get everyone out of here, ok?

ALAN: I'll go turn off the music.

MICHELE: And I'll start spreading the word to clear out.

JAIME: Thanks. I'll—

ALAN: (*Looking at the stairs and interrupting his brother*) Oh, no. Here comes trouble.

Both JAIME and MICHELE turn toward the stairs. WALKER, an older boy from the next town, is coming into the basement, followed by two of his friends. It is clear that they are drunk and it quickly becomes apparent that they are looking for trouble. MR. MASTERS is following them down the stairs, trying to stop them.

MR. MASTERS: (Shouting) Excuse me! I said, Excuse me. The party's over. Would you please leave?

WALKER and his friends ignore him. WALKER goes up to MICHELE.

WALKER: Well, well, well. Who do we have here? Aren't you that pretty little thing that works at the video store?

MICHELE: Hey, the party's over. Time to leave.

WALKER: Now, that's not an answer to my question. I'll ask you again. Are you—

JAIME: (*Stepping between them*) We all heard what you said. Listen, everybody's leaving, so, ah, would you and your buddies please do us a favor and take off, too?

WALKER: Oooh, this must be the boyfriend.

MR. MASTERS: (*Calling from the stairs*) If you don't get out now, I'm calling the cops.

WALKER: Ohhh, and that must be the daddy.

MR. MASTERS: That's it.

MR. MASTERS *leaves to call the police. By now, the rest of the people at the party have sensed trouble. Some have begun to leave and some have decided to stick around to see what is going to happen.*

WALKER: (*Sarcastically*) Oh no, I must be in trouble now. Daddy has gone to call the cops. (*Turning to his friends*) Hide me boys, the cops are coming.

MICHELE: Look, why don't you just leave?

WALKER: Oh, is the pretty lady now concerned about Walker and his friends? (WALKER *takes a step toward* MICHELE. JAIME *again steps in between them and braces himself for trouble.* ALAN *comes up in back of him and a few other boys at the party also make their presence known.* WALKER *looks around and decides that the odds are not in his favor. He has to find a way to get out of a fight without looking like a coward.*) Easy, easy, boyfriend. I just wanted to give your girl a little thank you hug, that's all. But if you and your graduation friends take exception to a thank you hug, that's cool. That's cool.

JAIME: Just get out, Walker.

WALKER: Well, if that's the way you feel, we're gone. (*He looks at his friends and signals for them to start leaving. They all start moving to the basement stairs.* JAIME *looks at* MICHELE. *He is glad there was no fight and is surprised that* WALKER *is leaving so easily. Then* WALKER *stops and turns to* JAIME.)

WALKER: Oh, I almost forgot. I wanted to give you a little graduation present before I left.

From under his jacket, WALKER *pulls out a nine-millimeter semiautomatic pistol. He points the gun at the ceiling and fires five shots. Everyone in the basement ducks for cover or falls to the floor.* WALKER *and his friends run up the stairs. Upstairs,* MRS. MASTERS *screams. We hear two more shots and glass breaking.*

JAIME: (*Shaken*) Is everyone all right? Did he shoot anyone?

ALAN: It looks like he just shot into the ceiling.

MR. AND MRS. MASTERS *come running down to the basement. In the distance a police siren is heard.*

MR. MASTERS: Jaime! Alan! Is everyone all right?

MRS. MASTERS: Oh my god, did he shoot anyone?

ALAN: He just shot into the ceiling, Dad. We're shaking, but we're ok.

MRS. MASTERS: He came up from the basement waving a gun. I screamed and he smiled and shot at the picture window.

MR. MASTERS: It's a miracle no one was hurt.

MRS. MASTERS: It's a miracle no one was killed!

MICHELE: (*Looking around the empty basement*) Well, that's one way to break up a party in a hurry.

MRS. MASTERS: Michele, it's not funny!

> MR. MASTERS *hears someone calling him from upstairs.*

MR. MASTERS: That must be the police. I'll go bring them down here. Everyone try to collect your thoughts so you know what to tell them.

> MR. MASTERS *hurries upstairs.* JAIME *puts his arm around* MICHELE, *and* ALAN *and his mother look up at the damaged ceiling. Slowly, the reality of what just happened to them begins to sink in.*

Discussion

1. Have the use of guns become a common extension of violence among teenagers, or is this an isolated incident?

2. What do you think prompts Walker to start shooting? If he wanted to cause trouble, why didn't he and his friends start a fight with Alan?

3. Could anything have been done to prevent this type of trouble from taking place?

4. Where do you think Walker got the gun? What do you think could be done to prevent young people from getting guns so easily?

The Evening News #3

Topic
juvenile rape

Character
Newsperson

NEWSPERSON *sits at an anchor desk and reads the story into a television camera.*

NEWSPERSON: The Annendale School District has just announced that three months ago a twelve-year-old girl was raped at the Annendale Junior High School. School officials explained that they were making the incident public after a three-month delay because legal issues concerning the identities of both the under-age victim and the under-age assailants prevented them from coming forward earlier.

According to a district spokesman, the rape occurred in the boys' locker room of the junior high school. Last November, two boys, ages thirteen and fourteen, dragged a twelve-year-old girl into the locker room and sexually abused her. The names of the children involved have not been released.

"This is a tragic situation," Superintendent James Hawkins said today at a hastily called news conference. "We have taken every step to ensure that the girl involved has received proper treatment. Because of the ages of all the children involved, this has become a matter for the family court. It's hard to believe that something like this could happen to our children."

Hawkins went on to explain that cameras have been installed in all lavatories and all locker rooms to prevent something like this from ever happening again.

Even though the school district claims that they did not make the incident public because of legal concerns, the mother of the victim believes otherwise. She claims that the district wanted to "save face" and wanted to avoid any possible lawsuits. Late this afternoon she said, "I have wanted the district to go public with this from the very beginning. Sure, I want to protect my daughter, but more importantly, I want to make sure that other girls in that school are protected! One of those boys still goes to school there! Who knows if he will try this again with someone else? Parents need to know that this is what is happening in the school where they send their children! It's a crime that the school district hasn't said anything before today!"

When confronted with these allegations, a lawyer for the school district explained that because the two alleged assailants were under age, their identities had to be strictly guarded. He said that the school district could not do anything to violate their rights.

"What about our rights?" shouted the president of the school district's parent organization. "What about the rights of our children who aren't criminals? This country is in deep trouble when it allows the rights of the criminal to take precedence over the rights of the victim. These boys should be in jail! They shouldn't be walking the halls of our schools! They are rapists!"

"They are our children," replied Superintendent Hawkins.

Discussion

1. Should the names of children under sixteen years old who commit crimes be released to the press? What about the names of victims who are under sixteen years old?

2. Why do you think that the names of both victims and criminals under the age of sixteen are not released?

3. Why did the girl's mother make this incident public? Why didn't the school district make it public earlier?

4. Explain the rights of an underage criminal in our society. Do you think that the rights of the criminal sometimes outweigh the rights of the victim? Explain.

5. How do you think that the boys in this scene should be punished?

Violence
& Solutions

Faces of Prejudice

Topic
roles of prejudice and violence in conflict resolution

Characters
Lydia Pace, a conflict resolution workshop leader
Four high school juniors:
  Beth
  Jeri
  Sean
  David

> LYDIA PACE *leads a workshop on violence in society, stressing the connection between violence and prejudice. She is speaking to a class of high school juniors.*

LYDIA: *(Reading)* "I look at the violence and see that it is rooted in fear, rooted in injustice, rooted in poverty, racism, sexism, ageism, homophobia—all of these are violence because all of them deny the basic humanity of our brothers and sisters and children in this village we call earth." So said Mr. Ted Quant, the executive director of the Twomey Center for Peace through Justice at Loyola University. Think about the name of his organizations for a minute—"Peace through Justice." What sort of peace do you think he is talking about?

BETH: World peace?

LYDIA: Ok. What else?

DAVID: Peace in this country?

LYDIA: What do you mean? What sort of peace?

DAVID: Between races?

LYDIA: Ok. What else? (*There is no response from the class*) What about peace in schools, or peace at home, or peace between you and your parents, or peace between a boyfriend and a girlfriend? Could those situations fit into his definition of "peace?"

Some of the members of the class nod.

JERI: Ok, so what's your point?

LYDIA: My point is that peace—and violence—could be global or personal. We have to learn ways to put an end to violence, whether it be between countries or between teenagers. We have to find new and creative ways to make peace. In order to do that, we first must examine the causes of violent behavior. What does Mr. Quant believe is a cause of violence?

SEAN: Injustice.

LYDIA: Good. And what causes injustice?

SEAN: All those things that you read in his quote—sexism, racism, ageism.

LYDIA: Right—the "isms."

DAVID: But you are talking about violence. I don't see the connection between someone getting fired from a job because they are too old and beating up old ladies.

LYDIA: Does anyone else see a possible connection between prejudice and violence?

BETH: Sure, look at the civil rights marches in the sixties. People were becoming violent over racism. Not too long ago, African-Americans used to be lynched in this country. If that isn't a connection between racism and violence, I don't know what is.

LYDIA: Excellent. Now, how about bringing the connection a little bit closer to your lives today?

JERI: What about violence and sexism?

LYDIA: Where do you see a connection there?

JERI: The way some boys treat their girlfriends. They curse at them, order them around, and hit them sometimes. That's violence.

DAVID: Not all guys hit their girlfriends, Jeri.

JERI: No, but a lot of them curse at them. I don't know about you, but I think that what they say can get pretty violent.

LYDIA: Any form of abuse, whether it is physical or verbal, is considered violent. What about examples that are not so obvious? What about everyday things people do that are based on prejudice and could lead to violence? (SEAN *raises his hand and then puts it down.* LYDIA *points to him*) You had a comment?

SEAN: No. It was stupid.

LYDIA: I'm sure it wasn't. Let's hear it.

SEAN: Well, when we were in junior high, there used to be this kid in school who was crippled. He walked funny and talked with a slur. He had...

LYDIA: Cerebral palsy?

SEAN: Yeah, right. Anyway, we used to make fun of him all the time. We used to call him names, imitate how he walked, laugh at him, and push him around. We didn't do anything really violent, but now that I look back on it, what we did must have hurt him a lot.

BETH: Yeah, I remember him. What was his name?

JERI: Larry, wasn't it? Larry Adams.

BETH: I can't believe what you guys used to do to him.

LYDIA: Why do you think you were so cruel to him?

SEAN: I don't know. I guess we thought it was fun.

JERI: Everyone did it. You just followed the crowd.

LYDIA: And that made it right? (*There is no answer*) Violence against people with disabilities is a real problem, especially with younger kids. Ok, time is almost up and I want you to do one more thing. Imagine you are at a party, with all your friends, and someone tells a joke that is offensive and racist. What do you do? Do you laugh? Do you laugh to be polite? Do you ignore the joke? Do you say that the joke wasn't funny because it was racist? How do you react to it? Don't tell me now, but take some time to think about it and write your answers down. We'll talk about them the next time we meet, ok? Time's up. See everybody next week.

Discussion

1. Why do you think that prejudice is so widespread in this country? In your community? In your school?

2. What evidence of prejudice do you find in your community? school? home? yourself?

3. Who is fighting for civil rights in our country today? Is any progress being made?

4. What do you think would motivate a person to make fun of someone with a disability?

5. What could you do to help end violence that stems from prejudice?

Hating Whomever You Choose

Topic
violence and religious bias

Characters
Judge Wagner
Rabbi Bouer
Mr. Wichert
Mrs. Wichert
John Wichert, their son
Abby Walker
Marie Walker, her daughter
Mr. Thomkins
Mrs. Thomkins
Allan Thomkins, their son
Officer Schwartz

> JUDGE WAGNER *is in a basement room of the courthouse, addressing the parents and their children. The three teenagers are sitting in the first row and their parents are seated in back of them. He begins by addressing the three teenagers. He speaks in a serious and professional tone.*

JUDGE: You are here because you are all fifteen years old or younger and you have been convicted of a bias-related crime. What each of you did was inexcusable and must be punished. But you are young and education must accompany that punishment. Today's class is the first of six that you and your parents must attend. It is part of our TRY program—Tolerance Rehabilitation for Youth. The court's goal is to make sure that when you leave this program you will think twice about your actions and consider their consequences. The first several classes will be taught by an old friend of mine and an experienced teacher. Rabbi Bouer, please come in. (*The* JUDGE *and the* RABBI *shake hands. As the* JUDGE *leaves, he adds*) All of you must listen well. That is your job for the next six days. It may mean the difference between a future full of hope or one that is...Well, let us leave it at that.

JUDGE WAGNER *leaves.* RABBI BOUER *does not appear very pleased to be there.*

RABBI: (*Looking at* JOHN) First off, you, with the black and gold hat, get it off. What kind of clown would wear such an ugly hat anyway? (*Walking over and picking up the hat*) Look at it. Little gold pictures of little men throwing little footballs around. (*Tossing it back to the boy.*) Grow up! (MARIE *laughs. He turn to her*) What are you laughing at? Look at you. Look at those construction boots! What did you do, just come over from the construction site on your coffee break? I mean, what kind of young lady would wear shoes designed for a three-hundred-and-fifty-pound man? (*Next he looks over to* ALLAN, *who is staring straight ahead, emotionless, doing his best to look tough.* ALLAN *has his head shaved. To* ALLAN) And you, Mr. Tough Guy. Not looking at anyone. Not saying a word. Sitting there glaring at the back wall with a head that looks like the butt of a shaved monkey! (ALLAN *flashes a look of anger at the* RABBI *and moves to get up to go after him. His father, from behind, grabs his shoulder and keeps him seated. The* RABBI *smiles at the attempt at violence*) What? You want to hit me? You want to punch me in the face? (ALLAN *nods slightly. To* JOHN) And you. What do you want to do to me?

JOHN: (*Meaning it*) Bash your head in.

RABBI: Good. Good. (*To* MARIE) And what about you, little lady? (MARIE *sneers, looks away, and refuses to answer*) I'll take that as a slap across the face. Good. (*Assuming a less hostile speaking voice in contrast to his forced, aggressive posturing*) And I want each of you to know and I want each of you to remember that when you turn sixteen, and you (*Pointing to* ALLAN) jump me for making fun of your hair, or you (*Pointing to* JOHN) bash my head in for criticizing your hat, or you (*Pointing to* MARIE) slap me for saying that your shoes were made for a three-hundred-and-fifty-pound construction worker, you will all be arrested for second-degree assault and put in jail.

JOHN: Yeah, but listen to how you were talking. You'd deserve it!

RABBI: I was rude to you. I insulted you. I made fun of you. You have every right in the world to be angry—even to hate me. But that's where your rights end. That's what you will all be learning over these next few days. Among other things, you will be learning that you are allowed to hate whomever you want but you're not allowed to act on that hate. You must learn to control yourself enough to do nothing.

MRS. WALKER: Wait a minute here. You just said my daughter looked like a construction worker. What do you expect her to do?

RABBI: I expect her to control her anger and to consider the consequences of her actions *before* she acts.

MRS. WALKER: But you insulted her!

RABBI: The fact is, Mrs. Walker, Marie is going to hate people during the course of her life. She has got to figure out how to deal with that hate so that she doesn't get into trouble or thrown in jail. We're getting ahead of ourselves. (*Looking through a folder*) Which of you two boys is John Wichert?

JOHN: I am.

RABBI: Are those your folks behind you, John?

JOHN: Yeah.

RABBI: Thank you for coming, Mr. and Mrs. Wichert. It is important that the parents take part in the program with their kids.

MR. WICHERT: (*With an attitude*) Why? He committed the crime. Why should I be punished with him? I think—

MRS. WICHERT: (*Interrupting*) Quiet, honey. I thought you said you were going to go along with this thing...for John.

RABBI: Mr. Wichert, please don't look at this part of the program as punishment. Look at it as a chance to learn more about your son and your family. Parents may not be the direct cause of their kids' bias or violent behavior, but they are often at the root of *why* their kids are prone to violence. Something is happening at home, at all of your homes, that is contributing to a problem. I'm here to help you learn about that problem and to help you work it out. Ok?

MR. WICHERT: Yeah, yeah.

RABBI: I'll take that as unqualified, if not exuberant, support. Now, John, please tell us why you are here.

JOHN: (*With an attitude*) The judge told me to be here.

RABBI: (*Patiently*) I mean, what was your crime?

JOHN: (*Mumbling*) Me and Allan were caught spray painting a building.

RABBI: Could you speak up please, John. What were you spray painting?

JOHN: A building.

RABBI: What kind of building?

JOHN: A synagogue.

RABBI: And Allan, what were you writing?

ALLAN: Uh, swastikas and stuff.

RABBI: And what stuff?

ALLAN: You know, like "Hitler Rules" and "Die Jews."

RABBI: I see. (*Controlling his anger*) And John, why were you writing these things?

JOHN: I don't know.

RABBI: You must have had a reason.

JOHN: I don't know. Like, swastikas are cool. Hitler is cool!

RABBI: But Allan, didn't you know that what you were doing was going to hurt a lot of people?

ALLAN: You know, you guys have to lighten up. We didn't hurt nobody or nothing. We didn't break no windows. We just drew a couple a pictures. We'll clean it off.

RABBI: What you boys did can't be cleaned off. What you boys did left deep scars in that community. Yes, we can clean off the stone, but crimes like this leave shadows on the hearts of those who saw it. (*After a pause*) Now, Marie, could you please tell us what brings you here?

MRS. WALKER: She didn't deface any buildings, Rabbi, or destroy anyone's property. She just wrote a few letters to a girl in school.

RABBI: Mrs. Walker, please let your daughter answer. To whom did you write these letters, Marie?

MARIE: To Shelley Klein.

RABBI: And what did these letters say? (*No answer*) What was in the letters? (*No answer*) Why were you writing to Shelley Klein?

MARIE: Because she stole my boyfriend. Ok, is that what you want to know?

RABBI: And why were you writing her letters?

MARIE: To tell her exactly what I thought of her—to tell her to get her ass away from Michael, Ok?

RABBI: What specifically did you say in these letters?

MARIE *does not answer.*

MRS. WALKER: Tell him, Marie.

MARIE: (*With an attitude*) You want to know what I said? I'll tell you what I said. I said, "Die Jew!" I said, "Stay away from my boyfriend, Jew bitch!" I said, "I am going to kill you and all the Jews I find if Michael doesn't come back to me!"

RABBI: Why were you calling her a Jew?

MARIE: I said her name was Klein, didn't I? Klein is a Jewish name. I wanted to get her mad. I wanted to get Michael back. I really didn't mean any of those things.

RABBI: Did you think that her family would be upset when they received these letters in the mail?

MRS. WALKER: She said that she didn't mean any of those things.

RABBI: Unfortunately, Mrs. Walker, Marie's intentions matter very little here. People say "I didn't mean it" all the time. But what matters is what they did, not what they meant!

MRS. WALKER: I see.

RABBI: Well, my time is almost up for today. Before I bring in Officer Schwartz to give you a tour of the jail in the courthouse, I want to give you some homework.

MARIE: Great, just what I need, more homework.

MRS. WALKER: Don't worry, honey, I'll help.

RABBI: You'll be doing your own assignment, Mrs. Walker. I'm giving work to both parents and kids.

MRS. WALKER: Oh.

RABBI: Actually, bias crimes don't have as much to do with bias as they have to do with self-esteem. I would like each of you to define the term "self-esteem" and to describe what it would be like to have low self-esteem.

MR. WICHERT: You want us to write all this down? I haven't written anything since high school.

RABBI: Please try, Mr. Wichert. I'm sure you will do your best. And tomorrow, after we discuss the idea of low self-esteem, we are going to watch Steven Spielberg's film *Schindler's List*. It's a film about the Jews in World War II and it might give some of you a better idea of what a swastika is, or what Hitler stood for, or what it means to be called a Jew. (OFFICER SCHWARTZ *enters*) I see that it's time for your tour of the facilities. Until tomorrow then. (*Exits*)

OFFICER: Ladies and gentlemen, please follow me through these doors. Keep your arms at your side and by no means engage in any conversations with the prisoners....

Discussion

1. What is meant by the term "tolerance rehabilitation?"

2. How does the Rabbi insult each teenager? Why does he do this? How would you have reacted had the Rabbi insulted you?

3. What will these teenagers be learning over the next few days? Do you agree with the Rabbi when he says, "You are allowed to hate whomever you want but you're not allowed to act on that hate"?

4. What crime did each teenager commit? What were their reasons? Why did they focus on the religion of their victims?

5. What homework assignment does the Rabbi give? Define "self-esteem." What do you think self-esteem has to do with bias crime?

Statute 2010

Topic
punishing adolescents

Characters
Judge Murray, Family Court judge
Jamie Walsh, a sixteen-year-old defendant
Mr. Walsh
Mrs. Walsh
Eileen Worth, Jamie's attorney

> JAMIE WALSH *has been found guilty of several misdemeanors. He is in Family Court with his parents to receive sentencing.*

JUDGE: Family Court of Orange County, California, is now in session for May 15, 2010. Counselor, do you have anything to say on behalf of your client?

WORTH: I do, your Honor.

JUDGE: Proceed.

WORTH: Your Honor, before you sentence Mr. Walsh this morning, I would like to bring to your attention several items that attest to his character which in turn may help you consider leniency.

JUDGE: Continue.

WORTH: Your Honor, here are five letters from Jamie's teachers, family members, and friends that describe their relationship to the defendant and how much he has positively influenced their lives. (*Places five letters in front of the* JUDGE *and allows the* JUDGE *to glance through them. The* JUDGE *shows no emotion while skimming the information*) Your Honor, here is Jamie's transcript from high school. You will notice that he is an average student with grades of seventy-five percent or higher. He has never gotten into trouble at school and he plans to attend college when he graduates next year. (*She gives the transcript to the* JUDGE) Finally, your Honor, I would just like to say that Jamie is aware of what he has done, he is sorry for the trouble he has caused, and he has pledged never to take part in any destructive activity again. His parents, you might note, have also agreed to pay for the damages. We urge you to take all this information into account before reaching your decision regarding punishment. Thank you.

MS. WORTH *resumes her seat. The* JUDGE *nods her head. The expression on her face indicates that she has not been persuaded.*

JUDGE: Thank you, Counselor. Unfortunately, the information you have provided the court is not sufficient, in my view, to ignore the recent law that has just been passed relating to cases such as this one. (*Pauses and looks at* JAMIE) You have admitted to vandalizing several buildings in town with graffiti, you have admitted to breaking the windshields on three cars that were parked on the main road, and you have admitted to spray painting several others. These are serious offenses. And, by looking at your record, I see that this is the third time you have been arrested for similar actions. Am I right?

JAMIE: Yes, your Honor.

JUDGE: Jamie, are you familiar with Statute 2010?

JAMIE: Yes, your Honor.

JUDGE: By law, the new penalty for repeat offenders of crimes such as the ones you have committed is public caning. Are you aware of that?

JAMIE: Yes.

JAMIE: Can you tell me any reason why you should not be considered under this new law?

JAMIE: I don't know...I...

JUDGE: Let me put it this way. Is there any reason why you should not be punished like anyone else who has admitted to such crimes? Are you special?

JAMIE: No, your Honor.

WORTH: Your Honor, I don't think that...

JUDGE: Excuse me, Counselor, I'm speaking to your client. Jamie, after reviewing all of the evidence and after listening to the pleas of leniency from your attorney, I'm afraid that I must sentence you with the maximum penalty the law now allows.

JAMIE: But your honor, caning is barbaric! Caning is cruel punishment. Caning is—

JUDGE: (*Finishing his last sentence*) The law, young man.

MR. WALSH: Your Honor, may I say something?

JUDGE: Go ahead, Mr. Walsh.

MR. WALSH: Thank you. My son did wrong. He admits it. We all know that when you make a mistake or break the law that you must be punished. Jamie knows he's not special. He knows that he must be punished like everyone else. It's just that we think that this new law, this Statute 2010, is not right. He should not be physically beaten for spray painting a few buildings. We have already said that we would pay to have them cleaned and that we would replace the broken windshields. What more do you want? Do you want to beat him, too?

JUDGE: Mr. Walsh, I understand you are upset. But there is nothing I can do. Statute 2010 was passed by the legislature as a reaction to the growing number of crimes against society perpetrated by our young people. The court and the community have been frustrated because we have both been unable to put a stop to this destructive behavior. We have seen that physical punishment, specifically caning, has been effective in reducing crime like this in other countries. Your elected officials have decided to give it a try here.

MR. WALSH: But it's wrong to subject my son to something like that!

JUDGE: I'm afraid that many of the people in this community would not agree with you, Mr. Walsh.

MR. WALSH: But, your Honor...

JUDGE: Mr. Walsh, you and I cannot debate the merits of Statute 2010 in this courtroom. All I can do is administer the law as it has been written, and, according to the law, I must sentence your son to six strokes from a bamboo rod, on his bare buttocks, in front of his parents or parent and a witness from the state. The punishment must be administered immediately after sentencing in a facility provided by the court and by a person trained in such administration. Jamie, please stand. (JAMIE *does so.*) Who will be accompanying him?

MR. WALSH: Just me, your Honor.

JUDGE: Very well. Would anyone like to add anything to these proceedings? (*No one replies.*) Ms. Worth, please lead Mr. Walsh and his son to my chambers. I will begin preparations. This court is dismissed.

JAMIE *and* MR. WALSH *reluctantly follow the* JUDGE *to her chambers.* MRS. WALSH *stays in her seat, crying quietly, as* MS. WORTH *tries to comfort her.*

Discussion

1. What does Statute 2010 state?

2. Do you agree with such punishment? Explain.

3. Would physical punishment deter anyone from committing certain crimes? Explain.

4. Are Mr. and Mrs. Walsh correct in debating with the judge regarding the merits of Statute 2010? Is Jaime's lawyer wrong for seeking leniency?

5. How do you feel about corporal punishment?

6. How would you react to this sentence if you were in Jaime's situation?

7. What punishment do you think is appropriate for Jaime? Explain.

176

Owning the Solution

Topic
mediation

Characters
Two guidance counselors in charge of the mediation program:
  Mr. Holt
  Ms. Arnold
Two sophomores who nearly had a fist fight in the cafeteria:
  John Hunter
  Kevin Klein

> MR. HOLT *and* MS. ARNOLD *meet with* JOHN *and*
> KEVIN *for the first time in the mediation room.* MR.
> HOLT *and* MS. ARNOLD *are explaining the process
> of mediation.*

ARNOLD: Hi, guys. I'm Ms. Arnold and this is Mr.
Holt. (*Both boys nod. Neither is pleased to be
there*) Your assistant principals suggested
that you contact us because of the fight you
almost had in the cafeteria yesterday. Is that
right?

Again, they both nod grudgingly.

HOLT: And you both agreed to participate in
mediation, correct? You are both here
willingly? (*The boys do not answer. To*
ARNOLD) They don't talk much, do they?

JOHN: (*Pointing at* KEVIN) He did all the talking he needed to do yesterday in the cafeteria.

KEVIN: (*Getting mad*) Calm down, John, and don't start all that bullshit again.

ARNOLD: Both of you need to calm down. We're not going to get anywhere with this unless you leave your attitudes outside. Ok? You will each have plenty of time to tell your stories.

Both glare straight ahead.

HOLT: Let me start by giving you a brief definition of "mediation." Basically, it's a process in which a third party acts as a type of go-between for two people who are in conflict.

ARNOLD: Mediators are not judges. They don't determine who is right or who is wrong. They try to help the two people who are having a problem find a solution themselves.

KEVIN: Great. I can't stand the guy and you expect me to work with him to find some sort of solution!

HOLT: We are not offering any miracles here. We are suggesting a way, other than fighting in the cafeteria, to solve the problem you two seem to be having. Let's quickly go over the steps you are going to follow in the process. First, we meet with you, like we're doing now, to make sure that you are here voluntarily.

JOHN: Does "voluntary" mean when your assistant principal "strongly suggests" you come to mediation if you want to avoid any complications with "outside parties"—such as our parents?

ARNOLD: That sounds voluntary to me.

JOHN: Whatever.

ARNOLD: Next, we will lay down some ground rules—like no interrupting, no cursing, no threats—

JOHN: But—

HOLT: (*An attempt at humor*) Sorry, no interrupting. Then, each of you gets to tell your version of the incident to a mediator.

ARNOLD: You'll be brought into separate rooms and you'll spill your guts.

HOLT: A mediator will paraphrase the story and summarize the main points.

ARNOLD: The mediators will then help you see the conflict as a shared *problem* that you both must work together to solve.

KEVIN: Good luck.

HOLT: Then, you'll brainstorm suggestions, find an amicable solution, and pledge to abide by it.

KEVIN: (*With an attitude*) What is this? The Boy Scouts of America or something? "I pledge to..."

HOLT: Listen, Kevin, mediation does not always work out. A lot depends on the attitude of the people involved. But what I can tell you is that a mediated solution is more likely to succeed—and your parents don't necessarily need to be involved.

ARNOLD: Look at it this way, guys, if this doesn't work, you can always beat the hell out of each other in the cafeteria next week and get suspended. How does that sound?

The boys don't respond. They shake their heads, trying to look as tough and disgusted as they possibly can.

HOLT: What I can promise you is that all the people working with you will be objective and neutral and that everything will remain confidential.

ARNOLD: Do you both understand the process?

They both nod.

HOLT: Do you both still agree to participate?

They do not answer.

ARNOLD: Let's put it this way. Whoever doesn't want to participate may now leave.

No one leaves.

HOLT: Good. Let's get started.

Discussion

1. Are the boys attending mediation willingly? Why do you think that this is important?

2. What has motivated the boys to attend mediation?

3. Why do you think that they do not want to involve their parents?

4. What is meant by the word "mediation"? Do you think that it can be an effective tool in preventing violence in schools? Explain.

5. Do you think that mediation will be successful for these boys? Explain.

6. Do you think that mediation would be successful for you if you found yourself in their situation? Explain.

Cultural Justice

Topic
solutions to youth violence

Characters
District Court Judge Allen
Tribal Judge James, an elder of the Thlawaa Tlingit Alaskan Nation
Two seventeen-year-old members of the Thlawaa Tlingit Nation:
    Jimmy Royce
    Nate Clark
Rob Harper, the boys' defense attorney
Susan Brunton, the prosecutor

> JIMMY ROYCE *and* TOM CLARK *have been found guilty of beating a pizza delivery man and of robbing him of $27. Today, they are to be sentenced by* JUDGE ALLEN *of the district court. An elder from the boys' tribe on Prince of Wales Island has asked to address the court.*

JUDGE ALLEN: Before I read the sentence, there has been a request made by Mr. James to address the court. Mr. James.

MR. JAMES: Your Honor, I am from the Thlawaa Tlingit Nation. In fact, I am considered by my people, much like you, to be a judge. I have come here today to explain how I would sentence these boys if this were a courtroom on Prince of Wales Island and they stood before me having been found guilty of this crime.

JUDGE ALLEN: Please proceed, Mr. James.

MR. JAMES: Your Honor, these boys are young, but they have been found guilty of robbing and beating a man, so they must be punished. They cannot hide behind their youth. However, in addition to punishment, they must learn from their mistake. There is still time for them to grow into responsible citizens. If I followed the laws of the Thlawaa Tlingit Nation, I would banish each boy for one year.

JUDGE ALLEN: Banish?

MR. JAMES: Yes. There are many uninhabited islands that my people have used as camps for centuries of hunting and fishing. I would banish each boy to a separate island for one year. We would, of course, check on them from time to time—but not very often. We would give them enough food to last for a few weeks, but they would be expected to eventually find food and shelter themselves. Even though this is a form of punishment, it is also a rite of purification, if you will.

JUDGE ALLEN: What do you mean that it is a "rite of purification?"

MR. JAMES: The two boys must spend their days and their nights focusing on inner reflection. They must reflect on their crime and reflect on their punishment. At the end of a year, they will have purified themselves and may return to society as positive and productive young men. So you see, your Honor, even though we would punish them, we would be teaching them at the same time.

JUDGE ALLEN: I see.

MR. JAMES: In fact, sir, I have come here ready to post $25,000 bond for each boy. We will take responsibility for their punishment and their rehabilitation. Your jails are crowded. This solution would serve both our purposes.

JUDGE ALLEN: Ms. Brunton, as prosecutor, do you have any objections?

BRUNTON: (*After conferring quietly with her partner*) No, your Honor.

HARPER: (*Upset*) Your Honor, I strongly object. You couldn't possibly be considering this proposal seriously, could you?

JUDGE ALLEN: And why not, Mr. Harper?

HARPER: Because you cannot adopt the laws of a specific culture or people in a court of law.

JUDGE ALLEN: But their laws seem pretty fair to me—

HARPER: You can't punish Alaskan natives under one set of laws and non-Alaskan natives under another set of laws. Justice cannot be cultural!

BRUNTON: It seems to me, your Honor, that justice is justice, no matter what culture you are from.

JUDGE ALLEN *surveys the courtroom. He has been faced with a dilemma that he doesn't want to solve without considering the options. He does have the authority to sentence people as he sees fit—or as "creatively" as he chooses. But he is bothered by the idea of "cultural justice." So, he does what most people would do in his position.*

JUDGE ALLEN: I will not make a ruling on this today. The sentencing will be postponed until next Monday at nine a.m. At that time, I will rule on Judge James's unique proposal. Court adjourned!

Discussion

1. What do you think about Mr. James's suggestion for punishing the boys?

2. Define "cultural justice." Do you think that it is a positive or negative idea? Explain.

3. What ruling do you think Judge Allen will offer? Why?

4. Which ruling would you offer if you were given the opportunity?

5. Do you think that cultural differences should be recognized in a court of law? Explain.

The Evening News

Topic
guns and teenagers

Character
Newsperson

> NEWSPERSON *sits at an anchor desk and reads the story into a television camera.*

NEWSPERSON: A fifteen-year-old girl from Austin, Texas, has been sentenced to spend four days in a wheelchair following the shooting of another fifteen-year-old girl last month. Family Court Judge Catherine Tobin said that Alison Tipton needs to see what life was like for her victim, who spent four weeks in a wheelchair following the incident.

According to police records, Alison Tipton was playing with her mother's .357-caliber pistol and was pointing it at the head of her friend, Layla Parks. The gun accidentally discharged, striking Layla in the forehead. Parks survived the shooting but was partially paralyzed and needed to use a wheelchair for approximately four weeks. The girl still needs to use a cane to walk.

"I know the girls were only playing," said Jeri Parks, Layla's mother, "but my daughter is now handicapped for life. These kids have to realize that guns are not toys. Layla and I don't want her punished. I just want her to realize the seriousness of her mistake."

Judge Tobin apparently agreed with Mrs. Parks. Instead of time in a detention center, Alison was sentenced to spend four days in a wheelchair, two days using a walker, and one day using a cane. "You will live your life for the next seven days as though you were Layla Parks. You will go to the bathroom using a wheelchair, you will go to the movies in a wheelchair, and you will ride to school each morning on the bus designated for handicapped students. Perhaps by the end of these seven days you will begin to see the world through the eyes of your victim."

Tobin also ordered Tipton to write an essay about her experience to be published in the school newspaper.

Discussion

1. Do you think that the judge's sentence will be effective? Was it too lenient? Explain.

2. How would you have punished Alison Tipton had you been the judge?

3. What do you think Layla Parks thinks about Alison's sentence?

4. Should Alison's mother also be held responsible in some way? Explain.

Index of Themes

More Resources for Helping Teens

ACTING IT OUT: 74 Short Plays for Starting Discussions with Teenagers

Joan Sturkie & Marsh Cassady, PhD

Paper, $21.95, 358 pages, 6" x 9", ISBN 0-89390-178-4

Getting teens to talk about their feelings and personal experiences can be frustrating. *Acting It Out* offers a new approach: Teens act out a short play, then discuss how the characters deal with the particular issue. Questions at the end of each drama help students articulate issues and feelings. These dramas address challenging subjects: abortion, suicide, child abuse, gangs, anorexia, home life, drugs. Issues are presented in a straightforward manner and your teens are encouraged to talk about them in the same way.

STREET SMARTS: Activities That Help Teenagers Take Care of Themselves

Dr. Michael Kirby

Paper, $29.95, 8½" x 11", 80 pages, ISBN 0-89390-331-0

Growing up. Teenagers start out in the relatively secure environment of home and school. Somehow they must learn how to make it in the more hazardous world of work and adulthood; they have to learn how to take care of themselves. This book examines the roadblocks in their way and helps them explore how to overcome them. Case studies, role-plays, and activities involve them in the process. A great resource for a variety of classrooms and small groups. Could be used as a course or as pick-and-choose activities. Includes permission to photocopy student handouts.